Philosophers on Education

*Six Essays on the Foundations
of Western Thought*

PHILOSOPHERS ON EDUCATION

Six Essays on the Foundations of Western Thought

Robert S. Brumbaugh
Yale University

Nathaniel M. Lawrence
Williams College

UNIVERSITY
PRESS OF
AMERICA

LANHAM • NEW YORK • LONDON

Copyright © 1986 by

University Press of America,® Inc.

4720 Boston Way
Lanham, MD 20706

3 Henrietta Street
London WC2E 8LU England

Printed in the United States of America

Copyright © 1963 by Robert S. Brumbaugh and Nathaniel M. Lawrence

Originally published by Houghton Mifflin Company, Boston

Library of Congress Cataloging in Publication Data

Brumbaugh, Robert Sherrick, 1918-
    Philosophers on education.

    Originally published: Boston : Houghton Mifflin,
c1963.
    Includes bibliographical references and index.
    1. Education—Philosophy—History.   I. Lawrence,
Nathaniel Morris, 1917-   .   II. Title.
LA21.B7   1986   370'.1   85-26341
ISBN 0-8191-5131-9 (pbk. : alk. paper)

This book is dedicated
to two fine teachers

Anna Trask Lawrence

and Aaron John Brumbaugh

Preface

The field work for this book was undertaken at two institutions, Yale University and New York State University College of Education at Plattsburgh. Both authors have used the materials embodied in this study for Master of Arts in Teaching courses at Yale. The courses were given at both the undergraduate and the graduate levels. In addition, Mr. Lawrence used approximately half of the material in a graduate course in philosophy of education during the summer of 1961 at Plattsburgh.

The chapters on Aristotle and Kant, and the Introduction and Conclusion are of solidly combined authorship. The chapters on Plato and Rousseau are dominantly the work of Mr. Brumbaugh; those on Dewey and Whitehead are largely assignable to Mr. Lawrence.

A book of this sort has many friends and helpers. The list begins with those teachers whose names generally have been forgotten, but whose immortality is secure. These are the teachers who not only teach superbly but also transfer their love of teaching to the next generation. To two who are not nameless this book is dedicated: Anna Trask Lawrence and Aaron John Brumbaugh. Professional encouragement has come from many, not the least of whom are the students who helped to put edge and point to the authors' thinking on educational philosophy. Among philosophers we owe a debt of gratitude to Alburey Castell of the University of Oregon for his insistent enthusiasm for the writing of such a study. Van Cleve Morris of Rutgers University read the entire manuscript with discernment and critical assistance. His careful questions and comments saved us from many obscurities and clumsy statements. Paul Kuntz of Grinnell College, in the middle of multiple labors of his own, read early drafts of the essays on Dewey and Whitehead with unparalleled precision and patience. He repeatedly performed the signal office of the good teacher: the eliciting at last of a clear idea from a tangle of fuddled statements. Every section of the manuscript has been read and checked by either Ada Brumbaugh or Mary Lawrence or by both. Stephen Stolzberg helped with the index.

Part of the cost for the preparation of the manuscript was defrayed by a grant from the 1900 Fund administered by Williams College.

Grateful acknowledgement is made here to the editor of *Educational Theory* for permission to reprint (in modified form) the essay entitled "Aristotle's Philosophy of Education" (IX, 1, January, 1959).

ROBERT S. BRUMBAUGH

NATHANIEL M. LAWRENCE

Contents

Philosophers on Education

*Six Essays on the Foundations
of Western Thought*

CHAPTER ONE

Introduction

I

Unless educational theory is to be mere technology, it must examine the fundamental assumptions about the nature of man and society which underlie educational practice. Educational theory which undertakes such study is, to that extent, philosophical.

If we ask what a curriculum should do or be in order to provide the greatest social awareness and adaptability for the student, we are opening a discussion on the technology of education. But suppose we ask instead, "*Should* a curriculum provide social awareness and adaptability? Are these good aims? Further, if they are good aims, are they proper *curricular* targets or do they belong elsewhere?" These questions will soon require us to think about education philosophically. Very shortly we will be led to questions about human nature, the social order, the physical world, the ways of knowing, the relation between knowledge and action, and so on.

A risk attaches to each of the two tendencies: technologists may plunge in, thoughtlessly, to gain some preconceived concrete end in the educational system, only to find that they have successfully accomplished a result which had not been carefully thought out in advance; philosophers of education, on the other hand, may get lost in grand abstractions filled with glittering generalities and endless debate, but with no concrete suggestions for getting the ideal job done. Neither approach, in short, can get very far without taking some counsel from the other.

It is the considered opinion of the authors of this book that the present era is one of highly efficient technology, including the imminent prospect of machine technology in education (automatic audio-visual devices, educational television, teaching machines, etc.), but that there may be a corresponding poverty in our capacity to ask the tough basic questions. We can either ask and answer these questions or pretend they aren't there. But if we pretend they aren't there, they will rise again to haunt us, when some educational disaster becomes sufficiently apparent. If fundamental notions about man, thought, nature, human nature, and so on, are strangers to us, we can only settle our differences by political force, economic pressure, or irrational persuasion. Education, then, does not receive reasonable treatment when intellect has been allowed to doze, unconcerned with basic issues; yet at the same time the educational system is exhorted to bring forth reasonable and responsible citizens.

None of our pressing problems can be solved swiftly or by the rehearsal of persistent platitudes. Inescapably, the disputants, if they continue to think, rather than merely to react, will find themselves discussing very basic questions. We do not have to take dramatic examples. Try asking yourself about the worth, meaning, and place of new methods of studying mathematics versus old ones, and you will soon find that you must talk about the relation between man and nature, and that you cannot avoid a theory of knowledge. Being challenged by the root problems in education is not an affliction confined to the professional teacher. If you are simply an honest citizen, can you make a serious statement about the need for more discipline in the schools without stopping to ask what on earth discipline means, what sort of social institution the school is, or why you are getting so excited about it? Of course you can; but does what you have said show the kind of maturity that you want our schools to develop in the new generation? Have you thought, at all, what assumptions you have made about the nature of young human beings; about the nature of the world they live in; about what things are important to pass on, and what attic trunks of heritage it may be good for our successors to jettison? If you have, you are already aware that to be intelligently interested in education is, necessarily, to be something of a philosopher; if you have not, stay with us for a time and see what some men who thought deeply on these matters have to say.

II

Philosophies of education usually can be summarized in formulas. The formulas become slogans, and the slogans are then misinterpreted, having been taken out of context, without suitable study. A final stage of deterioration comes when educational malpractice is supported by appeal to these compact slogan summaries. Here are some typical educational catchphrases which were intended to summarize — not to be substituted for — sustained reflection on educational philosophy: "All knowledge is recollection"; "Man is a rational animal"; "All education is rhythmic"; "Education must teach us to live close to nature"; "We learn by doing." What things have been done under these banners! These ideas, and others like them, are reconsidered in the present book, in terms of the comprehensive philosophies to which they belong. Our aim is to infuse life into the dead images of live ideas. The ideas are alive, awaiting use anew by each new teacher. But the images are only pictures on the mantel, occasionally noticed and dusted.

One point must be clear: A philosophy of education is different from a "position." Generally a position is a body of doctrine, more or less coherently drawn up. It is something like a party platform in politics: "We believe," etc. One reason why positions are bad is that they too often provide us with only emotional reasons for accepting them, rather than thoughtful reasons for considering them. The more penetrating a philosopher's insights in education, the more devoted are his followers. He stirs them by revealing things that were formerly unseen, and they somewhat deliriously accept all that he says, often not asking for reasons, even where reasons are given. It is much easier to follow a leader than it is to work with an idea.

The "positions" created by apostleship often come into conflict with one another, and in the warfare between the old and the new much is lost. Dewey, for example, for all his criticism of Plato, is in many ways much closer to Plato than he is to the votaries of "progressive education." Yet most of Dewey's supporters and all of his detractors are unaware that this is so. They are hypnotized by the sound of journalists repeating one another. Thus the battle comes to be fought out in adult picture and news magazines as to whether or not "Dewey's founding of the progressive movement has been of benefit to American education." Dewey didn't found the movement, was often critical of it, and several times laid it out by the heels. He had a sympathy for certain aspects of progressive education, nothing more. But the public has other ideas, and alas, so does much of the teaching profession.

One of the tasks of our study of philosophies of education is to rescue the formulas and familiar notions from the sloganeers. We have undertaken to give them life and meaning and to exhibit them as central in a community of ideas that make up educational philosophy. When they are presented in this way, these ideas are not easy to understand at all; they require effort and patience to be grasped in the way that the philosopher intended. The alternative to the easy slogan is hard thought.

III

We have chosen two philosophers from each of three critical periods in the history of education. Plato and Aristotle represent the classical conceptions; Rousseau and Kant represent the great period of the Enlightenment; Dewey and Whitehead write in the twentieth century and speak directly to the contemporary mind.

The classical philosophers are primarily concerned with what was in their time a new discovery: the human ability to grasp ideals and "forms" through the use of reason. To the relation between the forms and functions of things Plato brought the rare combination of poetic imagination and mathematical rigor. His brilliant student Aristotle, on the other hand, came to educational philosophy with the eye of the naturalist, the biologist, and the doctor.

In the eighteenth century the Enlightenment reached a high-water mark. The use of reason to understand the general laws of physical nature seemed to have achieved a clarity and precision which defied improvement. As a result, we find both Rousseau and Kant accepting a view of physical reality, conjectured by the scientific intelligence of the time, which is very different from the physical view of the world in the age of Plato and Aristotle. Their central concern is with the individual human being and his freedom. How can we explain, and how preserve, an inner personal dignity which seems a strange exception to the rest of merely mechanical nature, as nature is understood by science and molded by society? Rousseau is, like Plato, a poet, an introspective psychologist; he has an unerring intuition of the dangers that social artificiality pose to authentic selfhood. Rousseau opposes thought with feeling, passionately proclaiming the ideal of the free man as the aim of education. Kant, with the same aim in mind, gives us instead a carefully thought-out critique of the limits of scientific understanding, showing why we must always find complete determinism in the world of space and time, but freedom in our moral lives. Here there is an extraordinary diversity of approach to a common problem within a period: Rousseau writes, we will show, a *novel of education* in his *Émile;* Kant, on the other hand, provides a *didactic* and wholly *objective* theory of pedagogy in his lectures on education.

In the contemporary world, there is an attempt to bring together the vividness and romance that were part of the Greek view of reality and the precision that seventeenth-century science had attained in its analysis of nature as matter in motion. Changes in science itself showed that the clarity of the seventeenth-century view had been bought at the price of incompleteness; the great theories of evolution and relativity are based upon discoveries which forced scientists to accept an intimate interdependence of space and time, and a one-directional development of life through time. Dewey and Whitehead talk about *process*, where Plato and Aristotle were concerned with *substance* and *form*, Rousseau and Kant with *freedom* and *mechanistic necessity*. Yet between Whitehead and Dewey the same difference (within a common historical emphasis) appears that distinguished Rousseau and Kant, Plato and Aristotle, in earlier stages of the evolution of philosophy. Dewey is the New England boy brought up to appreciate the value of "gumption" in making a paying proposition out of a Vermont farm, through hard work, an alert mind, and a strong commitment to one's neighbors. Whitehead is more the Cambridge graduate, a prizer of civilizations, of the cultivated mind, and of creative genius. Both men are aware of the tight interconnectedness of things that once seemed separate; both are sensitive to the need for adapting unchanging forms to a time-immersed world where "all things flow." For neither man is nature a giant intricate clock, for all her regularity. Rather, nature is the context of life itself, and cannot be considered apart from life, which she brings forth and nourishes. But where Dewey is constantly aware of the human need for other people to talk with, the need of practical application to show what ideas mean and what they are worth, Whitehead is more sensitive to the silence and solitude that surround each individual being within the flow of time. For him the great problem of formal education is to prepare the individual for the unending task of self-education, through which alone a man's creative capacities can be released. Dewey is certain that a divorce of theory from practice is sterile, Whitehead insistent that a divorce of abstract intelligence from feeling is fatal to both. If we did not see them against the background of two millennia of history, the two men might seem to us at opposite poles; yet both are typical of our own century in what they think important, what they value, and what they presuppose about science, psychology, and society.

The great movements of ideas through history can be charted in many ways. We must think of their growth as a sequence of insight, critical contradiction, and reconciliation. The fact that we still share Plato's vision of what education ideally ought to be, and still are thinking through his problem of how to bring the actual closer to the ideal, shows that there would be a loss of vision and understanding if we tried to treat the idea of education statically, as a snapshot might freeze it in a passing moment. Ideas must tack and tack again to meet the changing winds of time and human ingenuity. If we judge their course by the windward or the leeward tack, they seem to sail in inconstant, even opposite, directions; it is only through time that it becomes clear that their shifts and changes of course are guided by a fixed ideal: the self-betterment of man.

CHAPTER TWO

Plato: *The Fundamental Principles of Education*

I

PLATONIC ORIGINS OF EDUCATIONAL THOUGHT

Plato's dialogues, because of their extraordinary quality of raising the right questions and identifying the important ideas relevant to their answers, have had more impact and influence on Western philosophy and Western educational theory than any other writings in these fields. Plato's works offer, therefore, a natural beginning for our discussion of the questions great philosophers have asked and the answers they proposed when they turned their attention to education. But it would certainly be a mistake to think of Plato solely in historical terms, for the Platonic dialogues are more widely read than any other philosophic works. From high school to graduate school or adult discussions of great books, most Americans make their first acquaintance with philosophy by way of Plato.[1]

Plato's ideas on the subject of education not only are found

---

[1] A. N. Whitehead remarks in *Process and Reality* (New York, Macmillan, 1929, and New York, Harper Torchbooks, 1960, p. 63) that "The safest general characterization of the European philosophical tradition is that it consists of a series of footnotes to Plato."

in his text as historical facts, but are, many of them, living doc-trines in constant use. In some cases they have become so much a part of our educational thinking and planning that we do not even see sensible alternatives to them. The use of dis-cussion method as part of instruction; the idea of a university as the highest point of a public system of educational institu-tions, primarily directed toward teaching and research; the division of levels of schools and curricula into elementary, secondary, and advanced; coeducation; the combination of physical with mental "education" on the pre-research level — all of these ideas, as well as many more, originated as Platonic concepts.

We are thus reminded not only that Plato was an unsur-passed philosopher and a brilliant author but that his practical vocation in life was that of an educator.[2] Plato's stature as a philosopher and his genius for practical embodiment of ideas in educational programs and institutions place him in the first rank in the history of education; he knows from experience what he is talking about, he cares about it, and he proposes to do something original with education.

Plato's work shows with peculiar clarity the important truth that we cannot completely separate discussion of "educa-tion" from a broader context of considerations and convictions. His insights make it clear that we are really involved in com-plex philosophic questions, not limited technical debate, when we suggest that more of science and less of the humanities be taught in our high schools (because we want to keep ahead of Russia); that certain standards of information must be met be-fore we allow students to follow their own individual projects and interests; that we need more "discipline" in our mathematics teaching (and therefore should use the School Mathematics Study Group approach); and so on. Our detailed and techni-

[2] His career began with Plato's giving up his ambition to be a poet or politician, in 399 B.C., in order to carry on the mission of inquiry of his hero, Socrates. In 387 the founding of the Academy, a new idea in Western higher education, involved Plato in the design and administra-tion of his school, which he continued to direct until the end of his life. In 367 an invitation to re-educate a young Syracusan dictator took Plato to Sicily and immersed him in political intrigue and adventure. When he died in 347, he was still finishing the *Laws*, a model civic code, with an entire Book (vii) devoted to education.

cal knowledge has increased so much in all fields that we have often had time for little else. We ignore the relation between limited decisions and ultimate principles so frequently that were it not for a small number of philosophers, among whom Plato is the first, we should have no one to keep us aware of the close interconnections between the practical problems of education and the philosophical study of human nature.

Because Plato regarded philosophy as an activity or pursuit shared by engaged minds, he said that a "textbook of philosophy" is of little use; it always gives the same answers, no matter what the reader asks. Taking Plato seriously on this point, we shall keep our outline presentation of his general philosophy to a minimum, as a simple background for the questions we want to ask him about education.[3]

II

PLATO'S PHILOSOPHY

Plato's philosophy brings together three important themes. The first is his view of philosophy as shared inquiry, as a search for self-knowledge and self-realization. He had been convinced by his teacher and hero, Socrates, that the human self is a far more mysterious thing than anyone up to that time had suspected. Plato's early philosophical writings are all dialogues, in which Socrates talks with leading politicians, educators, and citizens of his day about problems of human nature and human society. The second leading theme in Plato's philosophy is the discovery of form. The mathematicians of ancient Greece had developed an appreciation of the ability to reason "formally": to abstract and generalize, to talk about numbers and shapes "in general." Applying mathematics re-

[3] Plato is very explicit on the point in the *Seventh Letter*, 342A ff., *Phaedrus*, 277D, and, in passing, throughout the debates in which the Sophists would prefer to make long orations, but Socrates prefers a method of discussion. (In this note and hereafter, Platonic passages are cited by Stephanus page [the page number and location by letter within page of the edition of Plato's works by H. Stephanus, Paris, 1578]; these numbers are now used in all texts and translations, and the Steph. page is the standard form for citation of Plato.)

vealed many quantitative laws and patterns in nature and art and seemed to promise a whole new world of scientific discovery and precision. The third major theme in Plato's thought, mainly his own discovery, is that of the relation of form to value. We can see what this means when we look at a Platonic dialogue as an attempt to present some insight that is true, important, and beautiful. There has seldom been, in Western literature, a more meticulous attention to "literary form," in the interest of creating value. Socrates was concerned with ethical and psychological questions in his later life, and no doubt it was he who caused Plato to look for the relation of value to form. But it was Plato's contribution to recognize that ideals, goals, and criteria are ends to which form, in the sense of definite structure, is a means, and that ideals actually operate as causes in nature and human life. Plato saw that neither evaluating something nor describing it can be carried very far without the other.[4] As a result he refused to separate questions of "fact" from those of "value."

Inquiry

Plato learned two main ideas from Socrates. One concerned the difficulty and complexity of self-knowledge. Socrates was condemned to death in 399 B.C. for refusing to stop his public inquiry into moral, social, and political matters. He embarrassed his persecutors by refusing to escape when he had a chance, drank the prescribed fatal cup of hemlock, and died.[5] He was martyr to a frightened and stupid "people's government" that had little use for individual conscience. Plato, on the verge of a career as a young politician, was disillusioned by the unthinking conservatism that led to Socrates' death. He

---

[4] Indeed, the distinction itself is never sharply defined in classical philosophy.

[5] For a detailed life of Socrates, see A. E. Taylor's *Socrates* (Boston, Beacon, 1952; reprinted in paperback, New York, Anchor Books, 1953), and for an appraisal of his impact on Greek thought, F. M. Cornford's *Before and After Socrates* (Cambridge, Cambridge University Press, 1932). For a less favorable view, we have the comedy *The Clouds* of Aristophanes, available in various English translations, in which a reactionary poet makes his character "Socrates" personify everything new in education that threatens to upset the "good old ways."

turned to education as a means of instilling the passion for self-knowledge in the young citizens of Athens. Socrates' death and Plato's defense immortalized the ideal of independent thought.

Form

A second idea, less personally vivid but equally exciting, was the discovery we have mentioned, that one could study the formal features of things, apart from the things themselves. A hundred years before Plato, Pythagoras had begun to develop the science of "pure" mathematics, as opposed to accounting and computation.[6] We can deal with the number two itself without limiting this concept to a pair of fish or of countesses. Again, when we talk about "triangles," we recognize triangularity as a common form even though different *instances* of triangularity may be equilateral, isosceles, and scalene and may be made of chalk lines, stylus marks on wax, or bronze strips. This kind of generalization was still a novelty in Plato's time.[7] A certain historical imagination is needed to appreciate the excitement of the discovery of pure forms.[8] In our time the biological theory of evolution, the physical theory of relativity, and the existentialist theory of the unique human self have played roles similar to that of Plato's theory of forms, in forcing a reconsideration of human knowledge.

Plato's forms are the characteristics that give things their identities. Two chairs, for example, share the property or form of chairness; this is why we call them by the same name,

[6] This point is well put in A. N. Whitehead's appraisal in *Science and the Modern World* (New York, Macmillan, 1925, and New American Library, 1948), chap. ii, "Mathematics as an Element in the History of Thought."

[7] See the work of Sir Thomas Heath, *History of Greek Mathematics* (2 vols., Oxford, Oxford University Press, 1921).

[8] There is an interesting mixture of rigorous formal proof and metaphorical, imaginative exploration of space and number in "mathematics" in this stage. Geometry and arithmetic were *felt* to deal with a new world of mathematical *things*, and to give models very close to our concrete physical world of space and time. See R. S. Brumbaugh, *Plato's Mathematical Imagination* (Bloomington, Indiana University Press, 1954) for evidence on this point.

differentiating them from, say, bookcases.[9] Just as we recognize that two mathematical triangles have the same "form," which is common to both, a Platonist thinks of two persons or chairs as having a common "form" that makes them alike. These forms are not things in the sense of material objects in space and time; they are rather sets of general characteristics, which do not change. We cannot see or touch them, but we can recognize them by using our minds to compare and classify and generalize the concrete things about us that we *can* touch and see. Plato intends to say that the forms are actually present in things and therefore are not simply arbitrary ideas in human minds. I think and say that two chairs are alike because there is something essential and common in the chairs themselves which makes them alike. (This is a particularly important point to notice, because in later Western philosophical discussion Plato's "realism" is challenged, and such general concepts or forms as "chairness" or "triangularity" are treated, not as causes and forms *of things*, but rather as ideas *about things* in some human language or mind.)

Their mathematical ancestry suggests to us that Platonic forms may be thought of as structures; however, they are more than structures. The forms are also, in his view, ideals and criteria of value. Some chairs are better, as chairs, than others. Thus we might say, "That's a real chair," or "That's not really a chair," to indicate that although a common structure is recognizable, there are degrees of realizing the form of "chairness," and these degrees are degrees of worth. One of the most important things to notice about the Platonic forms is that they are related to each other in a definite system. Some forms include others: the form of "furniture," for example, includes the form of "chair." This means that if anything has the form

---

[9] "Plato's forms" is a phrase that simplifies a very complex historical and philosophical problem. These forms are identified because we need stable reference points to use in talking, thinking, creating, and evaluating. They operate causally both as goals and as limiting structures. In further support of this theme, see W. D. Ross, *Plato's Theory of Ideas* (Oxford, Oxford University Press, 1951). For a presentation of the present "traditional" interpretation of the theory, N. P. Stallknecht and R. S. Brumbaugh, *The Spirit of Western Philosophy* (New York, McKay, 1950), is a good example.

of chair, it also has the form of furniture. Some forms exclude others: odd and even, for example. Everything that has any form must also have all the other forms that include the one it has, and cannot have any of the other forms that are excluded by its own. Reasoning and logic consist in tracing these systematic connections among forms themselves; they apply to actual experience because each form, as it is realized, brings with it all of its systematic relations to the others. The forms are ordered in a rational system, which does not change, and we can "reason" by tracing their relations. For example, if the form of "furniture" includes the form of "chair," we recognize that all chairs are furniture. In the same way, if "number" is divided into "odd" and "even," and "odd" excludes "two," then "two" must be an even number.[10]

Value

Like the mathematicians, Socrates had directed his inquiries toward finding some common nature present in the objects of human knowledge, but Socrates chose as his objects the study of the things that men live by: instances of courage, temperance, or friendship. Plato, carrying on Socrates' concern with the human self, turned his attention to the underlying forms which are the causes of value.

Value seems always to require a form which is the basis of coherent order: Beauty requires organic pattern, virtue requires a harmonious relation of man's powers and faculties, truth requires a systematic coherence of steps in a proof or inquiry. These forms — virtue, truth, and beauty — therefore themselves are instances of a still higher form. The highest form in his system Plato calls the "good," the essence of all that is right, proper, and orderly.[11] This form must be, in

[10] This account of the forms as limits, each one of which puts anything that "shares" it in a whole system of relations with other things and the forms *they* share, is clearest in the *Phaedo*. It explains why logic can be applied to the ordinary world of sense-experience and causal connection.

[11] The relation of beauty to organic pattern as its necessary condition is clearest in the *Phaedrus;* virtue to harmony, in *Republic* iv; truth to the test of coherence, in *Republic* vi. The form of the good appears in *Republic* vi–vii.

some measure, present in all things, giving them that value which lures us into wanting to possess them or to know about them.

"Knowing" cannot be limited to objective description without evaluation, as the Pythagorean program of applying mathematics might suggest. On the contrary, our way of knowing involves looking for the purposes, goals, ideals, which give structures their significance. We always want to know *why* things have the shapes they do. In the case of the chair, and other artificial things, their "good" lies in how well they perform a certain useful function, and so we can relate them to the user and to their maker's intention. In inanimate nature —the world of crystals, stones, and stars — we wonder why the same patterns repeat so often: The reason a modern scientist gives is that patterns in nature tend toward those with minimum free energy; that is, they tend always to have a maximum symmetry, stability, and balance (crystals are a particularly good example). A Pythagorean scientist would regard this selection of stable shapes as involving a kind of goal or desire, an innate natural tendency in things. A modern philosopher might be willing to agree that we can *describe* it as a search by each thing for an arrangement and identity that will be stable. Similarly, with animals there is a certain nonreflective desire for immortality manifested in the instinct for preservation of the species. There is, even on a low level of life, an innate drive toward self-realization. In man, there emerges a vision of ideals, a drive toward self-transcendence.

On every level, knowledge of the goals of the things we encounter helps us to explain and understand their structures. Structures are the fixities and finalities of things, whether they be the arch that the bridge is, or the oak that the acorn will become. They stay just what they are, and they bring a system of limits and relations to the particulars they characterize. But if we were to restrict our idea of "forms" to structures detached from value or purpose, they would become unimportant and unintelligible. The conclusion drawn by Plato was that values are objective and knowable forms and that the realm of the ideal is in fact causally related to the realm of the actual, so that we cannot really separate "description" and "evaluation."

The Forms of Human Nature

As Plato brings together the themes of self-knowledge and form, human nature, or the soul, turns out to be as complex an entity as Socrates had suspected. It is at the same time able to recognize the world of forms, which does not change, and to be sensitive to the world of appearance and flow, which does. Human nature innately desires the good, but it is susceptible to sloth, triviality, and ignorance, which require that it reflect in order to know clearly what the good is. The "self" seems to be a complex of reason, ambition, and appetite, through which it thinks, wills, and senses. The ideal for human life is an effective harmony of these aspects of the soul, a harmony which produces a genuine human being — a person who senses his identity with the ideal form of man and thus realizes one kind of immortality. The soul has a sensitivity to unchanging patterns and to attractive goals; it has freedom to choose its own specific nature, within broad human limits which are the same for all men. It is interesting to note here that, although men share a set of powers, they are not necessarily equally gifted, nor do they equally realize their capacities. Excellence in personality means a balance of wisdom, courage, and temperance achieved by the use of intelligence in self-knowledge and self-appraisal. To quote Socrates: only an examined life is *worth* living.[12]

Plato's philosophy, then, requires the conception of the ideal forms at its very center. In a sense it is both an "idealism" and a "formalism." As an idealism it concentrates on the fact that actual things embody ideal things only imperfectly; one circle is a better circle than another, one man better than another. Better in respect of what? Better as a man. If we do not keep the notion of an ideal before us, we lose the capacity to evaluate at all. We certainly can't educate if we have no conception of when the educational process does well and when it does ill. Even the shabby educational ideal of the well-adjusted man who gets along with everybody — the organization man, as he is called — is an ideal of sorts. He is exemplified,

[12] *Apology*, particularly 38A.

in greater or less degree, in all actual "organization men." All valuation requires a standard, and most standards are ideals.

Plato's philosophy is also a formalism, for the ideals are themselves forms. They are not mere targets toward which things tend or aim. They are present in actual things, giving them the definite structure that the things have. Every actual thing incarnates many forms. Some of the forms, however, are not *essential* to the thing, that is, they do not give it its most important identity. A chair, for example, may embody rectangularity and brownness, but neither of these gives it its identity as a chair; that is given by the form of chairness. The same thing holds true of human nature; we should be able, if Plato is right, to recognize an essential form of man, which represents the true goals of life. According to Platonic doctrine, then, the problem of education, in whatever field, is that of bringing a latent awareness of ideal forms — a latent awareness which every man has — to as clear and high a level of realization as one's talents will permit. The happiness both of society and of the individual will, ultimately, depend on our success in getting and communicating a clear vision of essential form.

III

THE DIVIDED LINE: KNOWLEDGE AND THE CURRICULUM

From this summary of leading themes in Plato's overall philosophy, it will be clear that the attempt to isolate a "philosophy of education" from his dialogues is a difficult enterprise. Plato would agree completely with Dewey's comment that philosophy of education is the same thing as philosophy itself, broadly interpreted.[13]

Accordingly, we are lucky that Plato, in his *Republic*, gives us an outline of the stages of inquiry which constitute the form for both a good discussion and an effective education. Not only does he offer this outlined pattern in the abstract; he himself uses the pattern concretely in the development of the

[13] *Democracy and Education* (New York, Macmillan, 1916, p. 383).

discussions in the *Republic* itself. There are four levels in our effort to understand. "Knowledge" begins with motivation, with excitement and a desire to know. It proceeds through a stage of experimentation, in which we check our subjective feelings and notions against the experience of others and the public world. Then, still in search of clearer explanation, we must generalize, and look for laws and theories. Finally, in a successful inquiry, we come to recognize a form: to see an ideal or value that has been operative on each level of knowing, to which we have been attracted all along without any clear vision of its true nature.

It is true of the forms, as we have mentioned, that they are capable of being realized in individual instances, with either greater or less clarity. The tight deductive order of mathematical proof, which we may think of as a clear example of the form of knowledge, is certainly widely different in its accuracy, clarity, and generality from the fabrications of mythology. Yet mythology too, as it introduces some notions of causal order and temporal sequence into the world it claims to explain, has *some share* in the "form of knowledge" — though far less, perhaps, than mathematical proofs or scientific explanations have.

The *Republic* itself includes a treatment of the theory of education in considerable depth. It exemplifies a method of teaching, develops a theory of knowledge, outlines an educational curriculum, locates education in its social role, and gives an analysis of human nature. We will follow the method of the *Republic* in our own presentation, supplementing it by the special treatment of motivation, inquiry, and discussion offered in Plato's earlier dialogues, particularly the *Meno*.

In the *Republic* Socrates leads a discussion of "justice." What is a "just" man? What is a "just" society? Why are they both called "just"? In Book vi he explains that in a good society policy must be made by legislators who really know what their aims are, rather than by the practical "political technicians" of the day. As part of this explanation, Socrates asks Glaucon, Plato's brother, to visualize a vertical line divided into four parts, each representing a different degree of "clearness of knowledge." These four parts correspond to the four "levels" of knowledge mentioned above.[14] We will discuss them from bottom to top, in order.

Eikasia — *Hearsay and Fiction*

The bottom segment of Plato's line is "knowledge" that rests primarily on images and imagination. It is a world of story, myth, hearsay, and conjecture. The term suggests a kind of picture thinking, and evidently Plato has some notion that to "know" in this way is nothing more than "having a picture in my mind." *Eikasia* has a personal subjective quality, a vividness, and a romance to its imagery. For example, really to "see" what an abstract argument or proposition means to me as a unique individual, a "myth" is essential. But obviously this kind of thinking, for all its authenticity and color, is wholly unreliable when we compare it to the common-sense world of objects and techniques in space and time; a carpenter, not a poet, knows how to make a table. *Eikasia* has the lowest position on the divided line because we are arranging kinds of knowing in an order of clarity, objectivity, and genuine explanatory power. All the same, images and myths, imagination and fancy, are not to be scorned. Plato himself ends the *Republic* with a myth presenting his beliefs concerning human immortality, thus showing the need for imagery even at a very high level of understanding.

Pistis — *Grounded Belief and "Know-How"*

The second level of knowing is called *pistis*, testable belief as opposed to individual imagination. This is the stage of tech-

---

[14] *Republic* vi, 510A ff. For the present purpose, the reader may sketch or visualize a vertical line with four equal divisions, labeled, from bottom to top, *eikasia, pistis, dianoia,* and *noesis;* at the top of the line is *to agathon,* the form of the good. The actual directions for the diagram are complicated by the fact that Plato wants to show a similarity in level by having the line segments in analogical relation (*analogia* in Greek meant both "analogy" and "proportion"); but he wants an "inequality of length" to symbolize the differing clarity of knowledge of each type. To represent both well, we need two figures. For discussion, see Brumbaugh, *Plato's Mathematical Imagination,* pp. 91–104.

nique, of familiarity with how things behave. *Pistis* refers to a "public" world. Plato illustrates the difference between these two levels in the analogy of "The Cave." Here he pictures the bulk of mankind underground, fixed in their seats, watching the play of shadows at the end of a cave. For some the only reality lies in these images.[15] Others are able to turn and see the actual puppets whose firelit images are thrown on the cave wall. The puppets stand for the actual world, the shadows stand for the partial representation of that world which most men confine themselves to. Even this actual world is an incomplete vision of reality, however, which is only revealed to the philosopher who leaves the cave and stands at last confronting the sun, the source and sustainer of all that is. The sun, in this tale, represents the form of all forms, the good. We will see in a moment where "the good" stands in the ladder of knowledge.

Pistis is essentially know-how. It is what the mechanic has that Mrs. Jones does not. Mrs. Jones knows that her car shimmies. The mechanic will know how it happened. On the other hand, Mrs. Jones may know how the stew came to be good, and the mechanic only that it is good. Most practical knowledge is of this sort: "If I do so and so, then such and such happens." Plato calls this practical knack *empeirea*. We get

[15] There is no doubt that the lowest state is associated with dreaming, reverie, myth, and poetry. At the same time, the prisoners' betting and guessing at "which shadow will come next" underscores the isolation of each outline from any larger context, with a resulting identification of "causality" as "expected repeating sequence." We can reconcile these two characteristics, perhaps, by adding to Plato's myth the explicit suggestion that the puppeteers make up various "stories." Apparently no normal individual persists in merely *eikastic* knowledge; he at least makes contact, through society and technology, with a public world, more stable and less colorful than his shifting inner dreams. Not only does this assertion fit other observers' careful descriptions of a level of knowledge which contains a comparable plurality and immediacy, but it explains why, in Plato's diagrams bearing on hereditary ability, everyone seems to have enough "innate talent" to go beyond this level, so that only three degrees of intelligence are recognized as relevant, where otherwise we should expect four. The second of these considerations is much more controversial than the first, and hinges on interpreting *Republic* viii, 546A ff., as a diagram inspired by Pythagorean genetic theory. The point is discussed in Brumbaugh, *Plato's Mathematical Imagination*, pp. 140–141.

our word "empirical" from this Greek term, and we use it to refer to knowledge gained from experience. It is at the level of *pistis* that we first encounter the idea that if something is true, it is true for all men. "True for me" can only make sense at the level of individual imagination, *eikasia*.[16]

Dianoia — *Generalization and Knowing Why*

There is a third kind of knowledge, clearer than knowing *that* and knowing *how*. This Plato calls *dianoia*, which is a kind of knowing *why*. *Dianoia* is the kind of knowledge a scientist has of my television set, as opposed to that of the competent repairman. The repairman has a circuit diagram and tests each element and connection to see how it is working; why it works that way is clear only when we see the behavior of each part as a special case of general physical theory.[17] Mathematics is an ideal example of dianoetic explanation: Experiments, from now until eternity, might well make us *believe* that there is only one even prime number, and give us a technique for determining whether any given number was even and prime, but it takes a different kind of explanation to show that this must be true in every case, and why.[18] The *why* here is given

---

[16] The distinction comes out clearly in Plato's *Theaetetus*, a dialogue inquiring into the nature of knowledge. The Sophist Protagoras, according to Socrates, had argued that "what seems to me is true for me"; on that ground, each man would have a "truth" for himself. But the case clearly fails when Socrates asks whether what seems the right treatment to a layman or to a doctor is to be taken as more true.

[17] A modern account of the kind of thinking here called *dianoia* might take advantage of the frequent appearance of abstract combination tables in our science. The accountant who takes as given the multiplication table, the chemist who "begins with" the periodic table, the logician who sets out from his truth-table — each is clearly doing abstract explanatory thinking; but equally clearly, he is on a different level from the theoretician in each field who studies why the tables work and what the assumptions and laws are on which they rest. Plato himself pretty clearly knew about and used multiplication and other combination tables, but he seems not to have had them in mind as illustration of *dianoia*.

[18] The striking characteristic of some of our knowledge is that it is always and necessarily so. And there is no way to derive this kind of necessity and universality by simple series of observations or experiments: those would only tell us what in fact happened in a finite number of cases, if there were not some intimate and knowable connection between those cases and the "forms."

by deducing the solution to our question from the very general definitions and operations of the number system, which are found by "generalization" or "recognition of a form." *Dianoia* recognizes the unchanging types and laws that limit and control the behavior of actual objects and processes in the common-sense world of public space and time. The forms, as we have said, are the causes both of definiteness and order and also of value. *Dianoia* concentrates on the forms in the first of these roles. It finds general laws and descriptions but cannot, with its formal method, resolve questions of evaluation. For this a still more adequate recognition of "form" must be required.

Noesis — *Tested Theory and Evaluation*

The fourth segment of Plato's line is called *noesis;* this is the knowledge that has true certainty. This fourth kind of knowledge includes the certainty that we know, that our combination of theory and data has produced an answer that is a good one. Since *dianoia* is, as we have just seen, a method of explanation by deduction from general hypotheses, there can be more than one hypothesis that will "explain" a particular situation. If it is hard to imagine this in arithmetic, it is certainly easy in social science: Different presupposed definitions of human nature could all have some explanatory power.[19] One task of knowledge on this highest level is to examine these explanatory presuppositions. We want the best hypotheses. We want to know whether or not the hypothesis explains all the relevant facts it is supposed to explain. At this level we pursue ideals of clarity, universality, and simplicity, which are higher aims than that of just letting appearance speak for itself, or letting experience speak for itself, or even putting up a plausible theory. The whole explanatory enterprise is dominated by a desire to get the best possible understanding from a personal point of view, from a practical public point of view,

---

[19] When we read Book ii of the *Republic*, we find the possibility of alternative "hypotheses" in political science: "Justice" can be explained in one way on the "social contract" thesis that men are by nature aggressive, timid, and calculating; it can also be explained on the assumption (an "economic determinist" type of view) that they are greedy, benevolent, and cooperative.

from a theoretical point of view. It thus ends with an evaluation, and Plato puts the form of "the good," the criterion we have been using without clear awareness of it, at the very top of the line in his diagram.

To Agathon — *the Form of the Good*

The highest object of *noesis* in Plato's system is the form of the good, standing at the summit of the divided line. This is the form which is responsible for the value and attraction of the other forms, and which therefore holds together all of reality in systematic interconnection. Plato tries to explain the nature of this form to us in four ways. He thus follows his own prescription of the four levels through which any educational process must pass, if it is to be complete. He tells the myth of the cave, a story of progress from a world of deceptive shadows to one of clear light, and the good is like a vision of the sun. He uses the language of direct vision, describing the good as the highest point of the "intelligible world." He offers a diagram, the "divided line," which we have been discussing, to locate the good schematically. And finally he explains an ideal course of study which would be the method to follow for acquiring knowledge of the good. Evidently, the types of study fall on the four levels of knowledge of the divided line: myth, technique, diagram, and direct intuition. In this case, Plato evidently feels that to have adequate knowledge, all four levels must be represented.[20] The fourth level makes it possible for us to see mutual relevance in the lower three; but without them it would merely be brilliant speculation. Knowledge of the good is the ultimate lure for all education, but men vary in how far they will pursue it.

Plato's practice, from the early dialogues through the middle ones, is wholly consistent with this conclusion. An abstract argument is always presented in a situation where it has im-

[20] The correspondence here suggested is:

Account of the Good	*Level of the Line*	*Passage*
Myth of the cave	*Eikasia*	*Rep.* vii, 514A ff.
Ideal curriculum	*Pistis*	*Rep.* vii, 521C ff.
Divided line	*Dianoia*	*Rep.* vi, 509D ff.
Simile of the sun	*Noesis*	*Rep.* vi, 507 ff.

mediate social and practical bearing. An elegant if fantastic myth gives vividness to the march of argumentative abstraction, enlisting not only our concern in the public world of utility and forced decisions, but also our concern with the vivid private world of personal, subjective imagination.[21] Plato's late works, all recognize the fourth level, as they extend the inquiring work of the preceding dialogues into the other three levels.[22]

The account of the divided line brings out, in its discussion of degrees and dimensions of knowledge, the complexity of the human self and of the world we inhabit. The human self is at once a partially separate, changing, unique individual in space and time and a timeless being able to know laws that are universal, values that do not change. Our existence is a complex interplay of transitory adventure and awareness of eternal ideals, which we can partially realize.

There is an immediate implication for educational practice and educational theory. It would be a serious mistake to omit any dimension of human existence from either. Education, to be realistic, must combine the values of adventure, social activity, intellectual discipline, and vision of a moral ideal. For all of these are aspects of the human self, and all are parts of our cosmic environment, causally related to each other.[23]

[21] See, for instance, the myth of Er, on the subject of immortality in *Republic* x.

[22] This involves rather complex problems of interpretation of the controversial later dialogues. The *Parmenides,* for example, can be read as a proof that philosophy is not possible unless we can grasp the multiple kinds of "unity" that occur in being as parts of some systematic whole; see R. S. Brumbaugh, *Plato on the One* (New Haven, Yale University Press, 1961). The *Sophist* suggests that in discovering a "form" we need to agree on abstract descriptive concepts; the *Statesman* adds that we must see the form we are seeking as a goal related to operations and materials that are relevant. In the *Seventh Letter,* it is clear that "knowledge" comes only when we have and compare "images, names, and formulae" — corresponding, in that context, to levels of the three bottom segments of the line.

[23] We are all aware of the "pendulum effect" in educational history, by which we oscillate between unsatisfactory extreme positions, each of which has a legitimate goal in mind but sees it as exclusive of other equally important goals. This is what Whitehead would call the operation of "fallacies of misplaced concreteness" (see, for example, *Science and the Modern World,* chap. iii).

Unfortunately, it is much harder to keep all these demands in balance and in harmony than it is to think of one or two of them as parts of a modern theory. Of less importance is Plato's treatment of the social role of education and of the formal curriculum. The reasons should be obvious. The Athenian city-state of perhaps 10,000 free men is a society quite different from the modern nationalist state, with its scores of millions. As to the content of the curriculum, our knowledge has increased *exponentially*. The job of sifting, condensing, and arranging is vastly more complex.

IV

The Love of the Ideal

In following the pattern of inquiry suggested by the four segments of the divided line, we will start with *noesis*, at the very top level; here we should see a common ideal that links more special aims and aspects together. What is common to all civilized men, regardless of their differences in personality, profession, and worth, which makes them concerned with education, leading them to build schools, hire teachers, and buy books?[24]

That civilized people get excited about educational change is a fact of history. Controversy about education is an ancient phenomenon. We ourselves are now in the midst of a debate in America which surely would remind Plato of the Athens of his boyhood. The Athenian conservatives were hostile to the "progressive" ideas of the scientists and Sophists (a new professional group of teachers of law, rhetoric, and "culture"). One of the best, and bitterest, comedies written in Athens was Aristophanes' *Clouds*, a play about the new trends in education.[25] The execution of Plato's teacher, Socrates, on the

[24] The assumption we are making is that there is a single goal, human self-improvement, which underlies the diversity of means, dictated by common sense, at some particular time and place.

[25] In the *Clouds* Aristophanes follows the custom of taking some well-known public figure as his hero and making him represent everything that is ridiculous or radical in some new cultural development: educa-

charge of "corrupting young men," was at least in part an outgrowth of this same controversy. And we will find a similar concern in eighteenth-century France and Germany when we consider Rousseau and Kant.

Why the recurrent controversy? What difference does it really make to us whether our children are trained by efficient discipline or enthusiastic "projects"? The truth is, of course, that we want our children to be better than we are. But nevertheless, we want our achievements remembered and our ideas appreciated by them.

All mortal creatures love their young and protect them. In his *Symposium* Plato points out that the theory which the Sophists held, that "by nature" self-interest was a universal law, is contradicted by the self-sacrifice of human parents, and even of other animals. Created beings have an innate desire for immortality: for "possession and unending possession of the good"; they feel that their own immortality rests in part with their children, who are like themselves, and whose lives reach into the future beyond their own. All creativity has its roots in this desire to transcend our short careers in space and time. Parents, artists, statesmen, and scholars all create something of permanent value and love it because it expresses something of themselves which goes beyond their finite temporal existence, giving embodiment to some more permanent ideal.

This is the conclusion arrived at by Socrates in the *Symposium*, a charming dialogue in which Plato creates a series of speeches on the subject of "love," as seen by various speakers. His selection is interesting, since its range and order suggest the kind of discussion he envisaged for the Academy. Phaedrus, an admirer of poetry, speaks first; then a lawyer, next a doctor. Then Aristophanes, the comic poet, explains

---

tion for women, payment for jury service, city planning, the new literary techniques of Euripides. In the *Clouds*, first produced in 423 B.C., the hero is Socrates, who teaches a mad jumble of scientific atheism and shyster tricks of law. Socrates had already, then, gained some notoriety as an Athenian intellectual: He had been an enthusiastic student of the new Ionian science, had sought out chances to talk with the Sophists, and had probably already developed a technique of cross-examination that he used later. The effect of this comedy was to prejudice the public against Socrates through its confusion of his own notions with those of Sophistry; this prejudice was still operating at his trial, in 399.

love by a legend of "racial memory" of a human state when men were four-legged, barrel-shaped, and four-armed. Next Agathon, the tragic poet, speaks in a flowery encomium. Finally Socrates, claiming to have learned from an inspired prophetess, Diotima, sums up the discussion by tracing all love and desire to love of the good, coupled with the awareness of one's own mortality. The reader, then, who finds Socrates' answer too lofty can narrow his vision to look again at the other experts' speeches, to see whether a legal, clinical, or poetic explanation of why we are so concerned with education is, by itself, broad enough to do the job. He will find reasons in the dialogue for feeling all of these to be partially true, but none completely adequate.

V

MOTIVATION AND THE METHOD OF INQUIRY

The vision of love, creativity, and immortality is the ideal. From it we may derive criteria by which to judge the success of the different educational institutions, curricula, and methods that we devise. But for it to be effective, it must be related to the other levels of discussion to show what it means in terms of form, of society, of the individual. In the present section, we will return to the lowest stage.

What is an educational experience like, from the learner's point of view? Is there a need for engagement in a quest for self-improvement, a genuine and absorbed desire to know, if education is to make the student better? Must learning be by grasping truths for oneself? Or should we settle for a student who pays attention, retains information, practices exercises, and knows where he can find references and authorities that give him information? The way we measure what degree of educational effectiveness we have attained, the way we grade students, select materials, and conduct classes, depends, finally, on the way we picture "learning" as it goes on in the mind of the student. The professional teachers of Plato's time, the Sophists, held learning to be mainly a retention of information and the mastery of rhetoric in using information. The benefit for the student was instrumental, as a way to wealth or power. The student's state of mind was that of attentive memory, patient drill, for the sake of an external goal in his future. Socrates disagreed.[26] Aren't there aspirations and ideals of the student's inner self? Isn't self-realization intrinsically rewarding, without external prizes for motivation?

Socrates had been confused in the minds of some Athenians with the Sophists; Plato disabuses them in a brilliant dialogue which centers on the opposition of the two ideas of education. The *Meno*, which we analyze in some detail, is named for its respondent, a talented young man who has had the benefit of upper-class education at the hands of the Sophist, Gorgias. Visiting Athens, Meno encounters Socrates, and it becomes obvious that his Sophistication has not made him a really educated person. Plato describes Meno's changes in feeling as he tries to "learn" for himself, instead of merely remembering, thereby establishing motivation as coming either from within or not at all.[27]

It is obvious at the outset of Plato's dialogue that Meno has not been taught to be a good human being. He cannot generalize. He expects Socrates to tell him the answer to his question "Can virtue be taught?" He becomes discouraged and abusive when Socrates offers to help him inquire into the question. Yet he is clever, wealthy, unusually attractive: he is not unpromising material. "How can we possibly inquire into something neither of us knows?" asks Meno, when Socrates

[26] Sometimes one comes across uncritical admiration of the Sophists in books on education, where their challenge of old "absolutes," stress on "skills," and attention to "social adjustment" are treated as anticipations of our modern progressive education. But in fact, apart from developing the arts of language, most of their contribution was a negative one; and we do not believe, in the light of this, that the analogy is valid. The extant fragments are translated in K. Freeman, *Ancilla to the Pre-Socratic Philosophers* (Cambridge, Harvard University Press, 1948).

[27] A new edition, *Plato's Meno*, with text and notes by R. S. Bluck (Cambridge, Cambridge University Press, 1961) has just appeared. A defense of the present interpretation, locating the *Meno* in the context of Plato's thought and other works, will be found in R. S. Brumbaugh, *Plato for the Modern Age* (New York, Crowell-Collier, 1962, pp. 56–63).

will not give a simple answer to his question. "Even if we found it, we wouldn't know we had the answer!" And, indeed, if "knowledge" were only items of information in reference works, this would be true. Socrates responds with a myth, an experiment, and a general statement of the method of inquiry. There is a myth, he tells Meno, that all knowledge is recollection; the soul, "before it was a man," knew the natures and truths of all things, and has within it latent memories. When we inquire, we are trying to become clear about something which we already know. But it takes an effort to "remember," and unless some problem makes us want to recover this inner insight, we do not make the effort to inquire. There is, then, no way to impart knowledge mechanically, by filling a mind with facts as though it were a storage bin. The student must provide the motivation, and take an active part, if he is to "recall" any knowledge with an inner conviction that it is true. Socrates himself will not argue that all the details of this myth are true, but he is ready to defend the conclusion that we will be wiser and better if we do inquire than if we do not.

Plato's use of this myth in the *Meno* is a popular presentation of a point that is essential to his educational theory. The latent power of the soul to remember truths it has already seen corresponds to the mind's power to discern unchanging forms in the changing world it confronts. The comparison to trying to remember brings out well the feeling that a learning situation always has. For the forms are realized in things in different degrees of exactness and adequacy, and are "seen" by the human observer with more or less clarity, depending on his ability and training. "Knowing" is not, in Plato's view, a simple either-or relation, with the only alternatives "knowing" something or "not knowing" it. On the contrary, all of us "know" the forms in a dim and confused way — it is because we have some notion at the outset that there is a form of "virtue," for example, that we are motivated to inquire about it, and that we have a definite direction in our inquiry. Whether and how far Plato believed this doctrine of recollection literally is an interesting scholarly problem but irrelevant to the apparently novel and certainly correct conclusion that he drew: namely, that learning must begin with the student's desire to know; that it requires active attention for the student to have the feeling of "insight" or "recognition" that comes with "seeing" an answer; and that the basic capacities for educational progress must be present in the learner.

Meno "somehow likes what Socrates is saying." To convince him further, Socrates performs an experiment which has become a classical example of teaching method. A slave boy, who knows no geometry but thinks that doubling its sides will double the area of a square, is brought by leading questions to recognize that this is not the answer, then to "remember" that the square on the diagonal will be double the original square. The surprising thing about this performance, particularly for a modern teacher or student who has not appreciated Plato's intended Socrates-Gorgias contrast, is Meno's bewildered assurance that he has watched closely and seen that Socrates *has not "taught" the boy anything.* We feel that Meno was tricked, for Socrates certainly has used "leading questions" repeatedly, and diagrams as well. But the fact is that in Meno's limited sense of "teaching" as authoritative, external *instruction,* Socrates has not taught the boy the answer. The method Meno has in mind obviously won't account for the result; he may still distrust the myth of recollection, but he will have to admit that a student challenged to think for himself can learn by directed inquiry.

Socrates then suggests that he and Meno return to their question of what virtue is, but Meno insists that instead they return to *his* question, and ask if it can be taught. The method Socrates uses is "the method of hypothesis": given a problem, we see what general assumptions would lead to a solution; then we deduce and check the consequences of such generalizations. For example, if virtue were knowledge, it could be taught, and since virtue is good, any person who knew it would also embody it and therefore certainly would be willing to teach it. We thus find that, if virtue is knowledge, there should be teachers of it. Suppose that teaching is either by precept or by example. Gorgias and his student Meno are evident proof that the leading Sophists do not succeed by the method of precept: Gorgias, indeed, as Meno recalls, thinks none of them teaches virtue at all.

Here Plato has Anytus, the democratic leader who inspired the execution of Socrates, enter the discussion, for Anytus believes virtue is taught by example. Just as a child learns to speak Greek from the community, without a special tutor, so young Athenians learn to be good by following the example of gentlemen, and of the great men of Athens.[28] Socrates doubts this. For example, Pericles was not able to make either his sons or the Athenian public good through his example. If he had been, and was a good man himself, clearly the Athenian public would not have rejected his leadership after his many years in office![29] Anytus withdraws angrily, and Socrates and Meno are left with an inconclusive end to their discussion.

It is not hard to see that Plato intended to demonstrate for us that virtue can be taught neither by precept nor by example, but by the method used by Socrates. For during their conversation Meno does indeed seem to become (if only temporarily) wiser, more energetic, less vain, and "better."

Plato himself never forgot the educational significance of this Socratic discovery of freedom of the self, with its implication that true learning is founded on motivation. Throughout his work he indicates that the use of compulsion, pain, and fear as external motivation in education is immoral and worse than ineffectual, because it makes students dislike learning. For young students, education should begin as directed play. The suggestions for introducing youngsters to arithmetic, written into the educational statutes of the *Laws*, sound almost like a contemporary first-grade or kindergarten program. But the aim of secondary and higher education is excellence in the appreciation of form, i.e., the permanent laws and structures that govern individual persons and things.

Socrates' discovery that teaching must begin in the accepted challenge to inquire is one of his lasting contributions to

[28] Fully to appreciate the context of Greek discussions of education, society, and political theory, one needs a picture of the *polis*. H. Kitto, in *The Greeks* (Baltimore, Penguin Books, 1951), brings out vividly the engagement of the individual in his city; K. Freeman, *Greek City-States* (New York, 1950), has a fascinating series of case studies of various cities, showing the range of variation.

[29] The Greeks were clear and explicit in their hope that their sons would be better than their fathers. The failure of sons of great men is therefore a very effective argument that example can't teach virtue.

modern educational thought. The Platonic myths give a vivid picture of the love of inquiry as arising from a sense of incompleteness and desire. Plato envisions the soul in the context of a world that stretches far beyond our immediate environing space and time, a self which recognizes its freedom and responsibility for choice. In the following sections the reader should remember that "motivation" arises in this subjective self but reaches beyond itself in order to realize its latent potentialities: to know and to attain immortality.

VI

EDUCATION AND SOCIETY

In the present section we are concerned with a "public" or "social" self, and with "education" as a community affair, aimed at citizenship, technique, and social adaptation. Can we take such an objective view without denying the importance and right of each individual to his private self, and his own quest for excellence? Does the shaping of "the organization man" necessarily crush the soul beneath a weight of social pressure? For Plato this issue was not merely an abstract question but a vital personal one. As a young man he had seen his own relatives set up an interim dictatorship and become so power-mad that he indignantly refused their invitation to join them. He had seen the Athenian state under a shaky democratic government try and execute Socrates for insisting on the need to ask questions, even if the answers were not always the conventional patriotic ones the government wanted to hear. Did the Athenian city-state have either to fall into absolute obedience to the whim of the majority or else to become the scene of a struggle between powerful minorities?

Plato's effort to solve this problem is not simple and it does not always match our own ideas.[30] The problem can be stated

[30] A great deal of unappreciative criticism has recently been leveled at Plato; we suggest that R. B. Levinson's *In Defense of Plato* (Cambridge, Harvard University Press, 1953) be consulted before the student accepts as accurate any violently critical appraisal — or any translation or comment on contemporary context, such as that by K. R. Popper,

in a simple way, however. We strive, as a society, for the best possible state. As individuals, we strive for personal excellence. Must there be a conflict? Clearly there was, in the case of Socrates. What the state thought it most wanted of its citizens, unquestioning acceptance of its rule, was exactly counter to the life of inquiry necessary to an individual's self-development. So the state executed its finest citizen.

The Greek citizen or politician was even more committed than we are today to the notion that the function of society is to transmit tradition, to teach useful skills, and to shape character, so that younger students may fit in with the economic needs and political "common sense" of the community. Education as training in the interest of society, as a social institution less concerned with the demands of the ideal of human life than with the need for social stability, was part of the common sense of the day. In fact, "the state" made a powerful claim on the individual, since effective life in a community was understood to be a necessary part of civilized living. Moreover, loyalty to the state was one way in which, by identifying himself with something larger and more enduring, the individual could reach beyond his own finite life toward immortality. Yet "the state," as administered by a dictatorship of influential Athenian conservatives, Athenian democratic politicians, the military in Sparta, the dictator in Syracuse, or the Chamber of Commerce in Corinth, would certainly neither produce nor tolerate a truly excellent human individual. Was it a necessary consequence of society's nature that state and individual could not realize excellence together?

Only a clear analysis of the forms of state and individual could decide. In the *Republic* Plato gives his answer to this problem: The excesses of existing governments and the demand for mediocrity as the touchstone of "good social adjustment" in the local societies were not inevitable, but the result of unclear vision and errors in judgment as to the nature of the public good. The situation was correctable, Plato

---

in *The Open Society and Its Enemies* (Princeton, Princeton University Press, 1950). Popper is right in attacking totalitarian political theory but wrong in believing the theory he attacks has anything much to do with Plato's ideas.

argued. By a close attention to education, the society could further the virtue of its citizens, and they in turn could modify its traditions and institutions for the better.

Education is meant to serve both the state and the person. To the person it owes the opportunity for the best realization of his abilities. To the state it has the responsibility of developing citizens trained and happy in the roles whereby they carry on community life. A just state is one in which these roles are carried out by properly trained and motivated men. A just man is one in whom the various parts of his soul, his inner life, operate in the same harmonious way. Justice (the closest translation we can get for the Greek *dikē*) in both the individual and the state is the aim of education. Justice is *"each part performing its proper share"*; it is the ideal "form" for both the constitution of the state and the constitution of the individual. But, as we have seen, a "form" is capable of different degrees and, indeed, of different kinds, of approximation. We share a common "human nature," but there are individual differences — Plato thinks they may well be hereditary — which mean that our interests and aptitudes will differ. Could there be such a relation between state and individual that the social function of each person was exactly the one which he found most rewarding and would himself freely choose?

This depends, of course, on the relation of the ranges of individual differences and of specialized social functions. Plato analyzes the human self into three distinct "parts" (drives, dispositions, or interests). They are distinct, though *not separate*, for they can come into opposition with one another in the same situation. One of these "parts of the soul" is appetite; a second is "spirit," which we can think of as "ambition" plus a desire for competition and overt action; "reason" is the third. It is within every man's power to lead an intelligent life, in which he does not allow his desire for fame or fortune to run beyond all limits, creating inevitable unhappiness. But, given their physiques and innate tendencies of character, some will find their satisfaction in competitions and contests, others will rather prefer craftmanship or farming, while a third group will choose a life of intellectual inquiry and research. If we think of social "classes" in terms of function rather than accidental characteristics, such as property or family background, it turns out that there are also three such functional "classes" in a good state. There must be producers, protectors, and directors. Plato can now offer a solution to his problem, though it is one that runs radically counter to Greek thought and practice of the time: When each individual has a place in the social class which his interests and talents match, then justice is possible at the same time for the person as self and for the society as organic whole. The details involved in applying this theory were too complex and novel for Plato to develop thoroughly, but the *Republic* had done what it was meant to, and proved that, while the state is a super-organism with its own goal and individuality, there was no necessary conflict between the society and the individual. In a state which knew how to use talent for the general good, a truly good man would not be executed but would be a useful and respected citizen.[31]

To meet the needs of the three classes, a system of public education would have to be devised. The aims and content of this educational scheme occupy the central part of the *Republic*.

The *Republic* is thus the result of a critique of the idea of education as social adaptation (the conventional view) or as life adjustment (the Sophists' position). In a series of earlier dialogues between Plato's Socrates and the various leading Sophists and statesmen of the day, Plato had argued that adaptation should be realistic — and, in Plato's philosophy, the forms are a part of reality. Neither uncritical preservation of convention nor powerful control of tools for manipulating public opinion takes account of the true ends of state and individual. The "finishing school" approach of the Sophists, teaching graces and skills to an economic elite, seemed to Plato very unrealistic in its notion of adaptation.[32]

Education and applied intelligence can modify and serve

[31] *Republic* ii, iv. The analogy of state and individual and the differentiation of three functional classes occur in the latter book.

[32] A. E. Taylor (in his *Plato: the Man and His Work*, New York, Humanities Press, 1952) stresses the difference between the Sophists, who teach an *art* of living, and Socrates, who doubts that this can be done. The contrast may not be, however, between art and life, but between the arts the Sophists offer (rhetoric, etc., which are only means to further ends) and what Plato would accept as an art of living that gives a life intrinsic value.

society but such service can be exacted only where the social gains lead to the individual's self-betterment as well.[33] Life gains in vividness and authenticity from being lived in a *polis*. We share experience with our friends, argue in the assembly, applaud in the theater, march in the processions, and have conversations over a bowl of wine. This can enhance, not destroy, our individuality, in Plato's view. He would not understand an idea of education that posited an antagonism between self-realization and social effectiveness: the two are compatible in principle, and in practice can become so if we attend to improving education as a way of improving society.

What conclusions follow from this philosophic analysis? First, since education plays such a central part in society and since it is through education alone that individual ability and social function can be made to coincide, society should establish free public schools. This unprecedented notion, along with his insistence on the equality of women, alone would mark Plato as the great educational revolutionist of his time. Second, the Director of Education must be one of the most carefully chosen and respected officers of the state. In the *Republic*, the two tasks of the most talented and educated guardian class are legislation and education; the teacher and the legislator are the twin guardians of society. Third, socialization need not be destructive of individuality. Practice in social action will teach certain habits of cooperation and conformity, and perhaps in any actual state that Plato knew, those habits were fatal to self-realization. This, he says in one of the letters he wrote late in his life, is why he has not been an active politician, but an educator. But there is no necessity that forever keeps the good person and the good citizen from being the same, and perhaps this goal will be realized — if not in Athens, soon, then perhaps in some remoter time, in some more distant, foreign country.[34]

We may disagree with Plato's view that a culture or a community is a kind of living reality. We may think that the

---

[33] "And moreover . . . the state, if it once starts well, proceeds as it were in a cycle of growth. I mean that a sound nurture and education, if kept up creates good natures . . . and these . . . develop into better men than their predecessors." (*Republic* iv, 424A, Shorey Translation.)

[34] *Republic* vi, 499C–D.

conditions of modern civilization make socialization more opposed to individuality than an ancient Greek would have imagined. But we can hardly deny that some form of social effectiveness is a legitimate aim of education.

VII

THE CONCRETE CURRICULUM

Tracing the four aspects of knowledge which must be explored and combined if we are to have a good presentation of Platonic educational theory, we have discussed the ideal which gives us a concern for education, the vivid individual experience of motivation and wonder which is the necessary starting point of learning, and the social context in which education becomes a practice of skills for the art of life. Thus far in our examination we have discussed the ideas in Plato which are peculiar to Platonic idealism, the areas of agreement between Plato and modern existentialism, and the affinity between Plato and pragmatism. In the present section we will consider the subject matter of an ideal curriculum. This consideration emphasizes the *structure* — definite method, content, and order — of education, looking at the form of education from the standpoint of *dianoia*, the third level of the divided line. Here we expect to find Plato treating the problems, and perhaps sharing the insights, of liberal arts humanism.

The schools in the *Republic* are of three kinds. The elementary school provides a basic general education for everyone. A secondary school offers a more rigorous physical and intellectual training for students with special aptitude for and interest in military, civil service, research, and legislative work. And a center of higher education continues the training of a more highly selected group of students, who will become research scientists, educators, and legislators.[35]

Elementary education has as its content *musike*, a study of literature, music, and civics, and *gymnastike*, athletics and the

[35] The elementary school emerges from the discussion of Book ii; the other two are not treated in detail until Book vii.

dance. Its aim is to elicit love of grace and beauty, to develop the temperance of the student. "Temperance" is the virtue of moderation and self-control: the recognition that excess in pursuit of pleasure or of wealth is not only bad taste but self-defeating. If we cannot convince our producers and consumers that living graciously is different from luxury and conspicuous waste, creation of new wants and a constant desire to "have more" will make everyone in the community dissatisfied with his share of comfort and commodities. The result will be to upset the economic sanity of the state.[36]

The aim of the elementary level of schooling is to teach aesthetic and ethical value. This is to be taught by practice of graceful action and by study of great works of literature which combine excellence of style and form with plots and characters that excite the student's admiration and respect. Our students learn in part by imitation and inspiration: putting themselves in the place of tragic heroes, of their parents, of great athletes. And the tendency of actions to produce habits means that these students will grow to resemble the things they are imitating. This, Plato believes, imposes a need for the strictest selection and censorship. Far from being the humanist who believes that universality of appeal selects and preserves the best that has come from the past, Plato devotes two books of the *Republic* to criticizing Homer, whose epics were taught in elementary schools at that time as the supreme example of literature, and also as a civics text; Homer's *Iliad* played a role comparable to that of our Bible. The trouble with Homer is that he is able to persuade us, by the beauty of his poetry, that Achilles is a hero worthy of imitation. But Achilles, looked at through the more objective eyes of a Platonic ruler, is often hysterical, vindictive, greedy, undisciplined, and unreliable! The "idea of a gentleman" of the Homeric age was, Plato saw, unsuitable and ridiculous as a model for society of Plato's day.

Although he is willing to take issue with the most univer-

---

[36] One of the models of society in *Republic* ii was an "economic" state, in which wants constantly outran supplies; in the absence of an education that led to temperance, this would inevitably happen in a large society. Plato's later story of Atlantis, in his *Critias*, gives a picture of the large and prosperous state suddenly destroyed by an intemperance that its lack of educational institutions permitted.

sally accepted humanistic value-judgment of the day when he finds Homer unsuitable reading for students, Plato's awareness of the influence of environment on character and his appreciation of form do lead him into an extreme conservatism. He does not want his students to have any occasion for first-hand imitation of intemperance and illiberality, and he supposes that the directors of education can select an environment in which there will be no such temptation or opportunity. From the discoveries in music and poetry, in dancing and craftsmanship, of the past, he proposes to choose only the very best, and by rigid censorship to exclude whatever fails to embody the very highest excellence. By "best" he means *both* most satisfying aesthetically and most noble in ethical effect. Censorship, whether we call it by this name or simply talk about selecting educational materials, is a controversial topic, even now. There are few people who do not believe in some censorship. Shall we have fifth-graders read Henry Miller? The question of censorship is never one of "whether"; it is one of "how much." Like all modern psychologists, Plato believes that the early formative influences are the critical ones. Taking the whole picture into account, however, we feel it necessary to say that Plato here plays the role of classical humanist so vigorously that he is led into philosophic inconsistency. Modern humanism holds that we must not only respect the discoveries of form that are a high point of the past but also see that new forms are needed as culture goes on.[37]

The secondary school in the *Republic* is designed to test and train the intelligence of its students by "ten years of pure mathematics as a mental discipline." (In its context, since Plato seems to have been making several points by exaggeration, one is inclined to take both the ten-year period and the absolute purity of this prescription with several grains of salt,

[37] The strict censorship is proposed in *Republic* iii, and the notion recurs in an even stronger form in the *Laws*. For the general question, see *Versions of Censorship*, ed. J. McCormick and Mairi MacInnes (Chicago, Aldine, n.d., and New York, Anchor Books, 1962). Plato recognizes clearly enough, in *Republic* viii, 546A ff., that no state created in space and time will endure without change, but he still has a feeling that novelty brings with it a destruction of form. This, while true, is only half of the story.

though there is no doubt that the recommendation of mathematics as training in reasoning is quite seriously meant.)[38] They are to learn to look for the permanent patterns and forms by progressive study of arithmetic, plane geometry, solid geometry, theoretical astronomy, and harmonics (ratio theory). This training is intended to develop appreciation of truth as a value: precision, rigor, and consistency in the art of thinking.

From the brief description of the next level of education, it is clear that a primary reason for this discipline is for training in a general method of thinking, which must become automatic and ingrained before the student can go on to a higher education. No discipline should be spared in the training of men on whom the greatest responsibilities will rest. Executives and legislators must use intelligence; they cannot trust to mere guesswork or short-term "savvy" in their political actions. (As we have mentioned, the very technique of theory construction by postulated generalization was so new at this time that Plato felt considerable practice was needed to develop familiarity with it and confidence in it.) For the students who do not go on to higher education, and who are to be the army, civil service, public engineers, and police force, the training is not useless, for their problems are precisely those of applying legislative rules, given to them as axioms, to particular situations, without contradictions or inconsistencies in the deduced application. This notion of teaching a method of thought is an attractive idea, and one that has enlisted many defenders in later educational theory. But it supposes that study of empty

[38] Plato is apparently concerned, in *Republic* v and vi, to give his reader some notion of the vast distance separating true temperance, courage, and wisdom from what passed for these virtues among the Athenians of his day. It is here that he insists that the "truly temperate" society would be one in which no man of the two upper classes had any private interest — property, children, or wife of his own — which he might be tempted to put ahead of the public welfare. And we could avoid any chance of timidity by raising children amid scenes of battle — a more rigorous toughening than the Spartans had ever advocated. As a continuation of this same line of argument, we must give legislative power to philosophers, who have been trained to disregard all empiricism. Whatever the exact intention of these "three waves of argument," it does seem clear that Plato intends to startle his reader, and probably for that purpose indulges in some exaggeration. One sign of this is that if we take the section literally, it will not square with other parts of the *Republic* itself.

pattern will be interesting, applicable to life, and automatically transferable; and experience has tended to cast doubt on each of these claims. The dialogues after the *Republic* find Plato reconsidering or reinterpreting this curricular proposal, as he criticizes formal logic for its tendency to pay attention to structure without content and form.[39]

The higher education, for future legislators, will consist of "dialectic." Dialectic is a term with a varied history of meanings, and Plato himself uses it sometimes in the informal sense of directed conversation, sometimes as naming a practical method of inquiry, sometimes for logical precision in defining and classifying.[40] Glaucon asks Socrates to tell him what "dialectic" is, but the answer is rather sketchy. However, if all students are to pursue this as their single course, it is clear that Plato's idea of "subject matter" on this level is not at all our own notion of departmentalization within the college and division into professional schools within the university. We

[39] Plato had already remarked, in *Republic* vii, that mathematicians are not always good philosophers. In the *Theaetetus*, the characterization of Theodorus, the old and eminent mathematician who never connected his mathematics with the "abstract arguments" of philosophy, illustrates the point dramatically.

The opening scene of the *Parmenides* offers a vivid contrast between the young men who see "mental gymnastic" as an end in itself, offering exercise and competition, and others who can appreciate it as related to philosophy proper. See Brumbaugh, *Plato on the One*, pp. 26–33.

Although, in the *Sophist* and *Statesman*, the definitions are said to be undertaken only as examples of a method that will make young men better dialecticians, the running metaphor of the hunt and the hunter hunted, in the former, and of the divine and human craftsman, in the latter, in fact keep methodology focused in each case on a further philosophical objective and function.

In the *Philebus*, evaluation involves recognition of measure; pure mathematics, without its applied counterpart, is not adequate for a human life, nor for determining good measures. In fact, pure mathematics without application would be ridiculous, for the pure mathematician could not even find his way home. And the class of the finite, which pure mathematics seems to study, is to be related to measure as a higher normative category; symmetry is only one of the "touchstones of the good." In *Laws* vii there is a clear application of this principle to education, where the central mathematical content is to be commensurability and measure. This does not give up pure mathematics but connects it more tightly with motivation and social uses. Plato still thinks the study of incommensurables in solids would be an excellent leisure occupation for the elder citizens of the state.

[40] All of these uses will be found under *dialegō, dialektikē*, in F. Ast's *Lexikon Platonicum*, 3 vols. (Leipzig, 1835).

44   *The Fundamental Principles of Education*

do get several pieces of information about the intended course, and by putting them together we can see why Plato left the details so incomplete in his discussion of curriculum.[41]

It seems evident that Plato here thinks of dialectic as an application of the clear, logical methods of mathematics to the tangled phenomena of human nature and conduct.[42] The result would be, if this program were carried out, an inquiry into such concepts as "justice," on the pattern of the "divided line." And it has been shown in recent studies that precisely such an inquiry is what is carried on in Books i–iv of the *Republic* itself.[43] In those books we begin with hearsay, move through the level of experience, and encounter two conflicting "general hypotheses" about the nature of society. The conflict between these is resolved by including both in a still more general and adequate "theory," the consequences and presuppositions of which develop in the following discussion. There is no need, therefore, for an elaborate description of dialectic in *Republic* vii, since we already have a demonstration of it in action, in the *Republic* itself.[44]

[41] *Republic* vii.

[42] The idea of applying mathematical methods to political affairs seems to have been Pythagorean. We find it in the fragments of Archytas, an eminent statesman and mathematician of Tarentum whom Plato visited just before founding the Academy. The influence of Archytas on Plato is generally agreed upon; he is sometimes thought to be the model of Plato's "philosopher-king" in the *Republic*. For an account of him, and the fragments attributed to him (which recent scholarship tends to accept as genuine), see K. Freeman, *Ancilla to the Pre-Socratic Philosophers*, and *The Pre-Socratic Philosophers* (Cambridge, Harvard University Press, 1947). For his relation to Plato, see P.-M. Schuhl, *L'Oeuvre de Platon* (Paris, 1954), and Brumbaugh, *Plato for the Modern Age*, pp. 77–78.

[43] This was developed independently by R. S. Brumbaugh (*Plato's Mathematical Imagination*, p. 101, fig. 43; *Plato on the One*, pp. 195–197) and Paul Desjardins ("The Form of Platonic Inquiry," Ph.D. dissertation, Yale, 1957).

[44] The suggested equivalence of speakers and levels is:

eikasia: Cephalus and his son Polemarchus.
pistis: Thrasymachus, who has legal experience and "know-how" but does not get to a general theory.
dianoia: Glaucon and Adeimantus, who develop a "social contract" hypothesis as a theoretical explanation of Thrasymachus' rather dour observations.
noesis: Socrates, who is able to show that the "social contract" is an incomplete generalization, explaining only a part of human behavior, and who includes it within his more complete theory.

Beyond skill in dialectic lies the vision of the good, the end of all philosophic understanding. The idea of the good permeates all the levels of understanding, providing them with that worth which lures us to self-realization by our knowledge of them. Plato says of this form of all forms that it is like the sun. The sun is the ultimate source of light by which actual things are seen — that is, are known and apprehended. It also sustains them in their very existence. So also the good is what illuminates what we *understand*, and the very reality of these things is dependent upon it.

"The good" is one of Plato's most difficult ideas, and volumes have been written about it.[45] For our purposes it stands as the apex of value, upon which all other value depends. The educational development of men depends on how far their talents and motivation carry them toward this highest vision. Plato's highest judgment seems to have been that this vision cannot be translated into a doctrine and presented in textbook or lecture form, though the route of inquiry may be marked out.

Notice that Plato's idea of higher education is one of synthesis, not of specialization. Just as, in the *Symposium*, poets, doctors, and lawyers are brought together in an attempt to synthesize their observations and notions into an adequate account of the nature of "love," so the higher learning is to be practiced in appreciating and ordering general and expert findings into unified theories. If there is to be research into details of medicine, mathematics, law, or zoology, it should come later, so that the scholar has constantly before his mind the ideal of knowledge and can use it as a criterion of importance in his work on detail.[46]

[45] The doctrines taught in the latest phase of the Academy remain unclear. Aristotle, our main source on the point, seems to select and restate, for purposes of his own philosophic argument. See the final chapter of Taylor's *Plato;* W. D. Ross, *Aristotle: Select Fragments* (vol. xii of the Oxford translation, Oxford, Oxford University Press, 1952); P. Merlan, *From Platonism to Neo-Platonism* (The Hague, 1959).

[46] An interesting illustration is the treatment of medicine and psychology in Plato's *Timaeus*. This dialogue seems to be the Academy's encyclopedia of what was known in the natural sciences; its medical section is carefully worked out and was used (out of context) as a textbook in later medical tradition. But looked at as an Academic handbook of medicine, this shows clearly how much a young doctor should

Platonic education is thus a training in what he would call "philosophy" and "philosophic vision." In American higher education today we are still concerned with this question. Should college, all of it, or at least the first two years, be devoted to giving the student a "general education"? If so, can this best be done by wide sampling of detailed courses in different "areas," or by specially designed "survey" or "general" courses that cross traditional departmental boundaries? Is the "major" for undergraduate upperclassmen to be considered specialized preprofessional training or a continuation of less specialized liberal education? Is there any necessity for "major" fields to coincide with the existing departments, or should there be flexibility in providing for "divisional" or "interdepartmental" study here? These are vital, immediate questions, and, by implication, they are also important for secondary education. If high school education is to be terminal for some students, does this mean that there should also be some attention to synthesis and synoptic vision on this level? Or is the best we can attain merely competence in socialization and in those instrumental techniques that a citizen needs in order to be "adapted" and "effective"?

There are similar questions posed by the high school and elementary school curricula Plato proposed. As these questions are raised by later educational philosophers, we will have an opportunity to discuss them in the course of the following chapters. For the present, we can summarize Plato's curricular plan by noticing that it is intended to develop each individual's intellectual powers to choose formal studies which will best make him aware of the beautiful, the good, and the true.

---

know (politics, cosmology, inorganic chemistry, among other things) before he can judiciously "specialize." The Hippocratic doctors, who tended toward specialization and away from so much superstructure, are criticized for bad diagnoses resulting from their ignoring the close relation of medicine to ethics and psychology. The same moral, this time for lawyers and legislators, comes out in the amount of philosophical background material included in Plato's *Laws*.

VIII

Conclusion

We end our conversation with Plato where we began: with the vision of an ideal of harmony and human self-realization awaiting us for its concrete realization in a complex human situation which exists with one pole of the self akin to eternity, the other immersed in the flow of time.

It is time now to invite some later philosophers to our modern Academic symposium. We will find that their treatments of education are shaped by the fundamental questions Plato has presented. But it is important to see both what the results are of more detailed explorations of such ideas as growth, freedom, and form, and what changes and new interpretations are required to take account of our progress since Plato's day. It is surprising how much progress there has been in the development of democratic society, of technology, of ethical sensitivity, of teaching techniques in some subject matters. For example, long division is no longer an obscure mystery, requiring special courses in advanced computation; and we no longer need to depend on slave labor as the only available power source for public works. Study of heredity and environment suggests that all or most men have the potential ability to benefit from secondary and higher education and to share in the social functions of legislation, production, and protection.

As we look at later philosophers treating education, we will find that each thinker we have chosen offers some distinctive clarification or proposes an essential revision of Plato's scheme. Aristotle clarifies the ideas of causality and growth. Rousseau revises the classical concept of human nature and points out some of the inherent dangers in society. Kant enlarges the notions of freedom and responsibility and their implication for education. Dewey completely revises the classical notion of class structure in society and correctly criticizes many "dualistic" ways of thought. Whitehead underscores the importance of creativity and sensitivity to immediate experience. But the ideal of discovering clearly the form and aims of education still remains a challenging enterprise, left as a heritage by Plato.

Suggestions for Further Reading

The best way to learn about Plato is to read his *Dialogues* themselves. The standard English translation of B. Jowett (*The Dialogues of Plato*, 3rd ed., Oxford, 1920, and New York, Random House, 2 vols., 1937) is particularly good for the earlier dialogues. *The Collected Dialogues of Plato*, in various translations, edited by Edith Hamilton and Huntington Cairns (New York, Pantheon Books, 1961), includes the important *Seventh Letter* and a selection of versions of the later dialogues often more accurate than Jowett's translation.

Secondary sources include: A. E. Taylor, *Plato: the Man and His Work* (6th ed., New York, Humanities Press, 1952), A. Koyré, *Discovering Plato*, trans. L. C. Rosenfeld (New York, Columbia University Press, 1960), R. S. Bluck, *Plato's Life and Thought* (Boston, Beacon, 1951), G. C. Field, *Philosophy of Plato* (Oxford, Oxford University Press, 1949), R. S. Brumbaugh, *Plato for the Modern Age* (New York, Crowell-Collier, 1962). The last of these has a bibliography, with annotation, of recent books and articles in English that will serve as a guide for the reader who wants to follow some specific dialogue or topic further. See also the "Plato" articles in the *Encyclopaedia Britannica* (11th ed.), by A. E. Taylor, and the *Encyclopedia Americana* (1962 revision), by R. S. Brumbaugh.

Of particular interest for the philosophy of education is R. C. Lodge, *Plato's Theory of Education* (New York, Harcourt, Brace, 1947). In addition, there are two scholarly studies which every student of Greek educational theory should know. These are Werner Jaeger's *Paideia*, 3 vols. (trans. G. Highet, New York, Oxford University Press, 1939), and P. Friedländer's *Plato*, currently being translated into English by Hans Meyerhoff. Vol. I has already appeared (New York, Pantheon Books, 1958).

CHAPTER THREE

Aristotle: *Education as Self-Realization*

I

INTRODUCTION

One of the arresting contrasts in the history of Western philosophy is that between Plato and his most brilliant student, Aristotle. After Aristotle left Plato's Academy he became the tutor of Alexander the Great. Later he founded a school of his own, the "Lyceum," which rivaled the Academy in Athens. He developed his own philosophy, which has ever since competed with that of Plato. One principal difference in the two men is that, where Plato showed particular interest in higher mathematics and poetry, Aristotle tended rather to take his examples from biology, medicine, and technology. From his early Academy years, Aristotle seems to have wanted to connect and test Plato's insights with a public world of common sense and experimental fact. The difference in temperament between the two men is indicated in Coleridge's remark that every man was born either a Platonist or an Aristotelian.[1]

Where Plato wrote dramatic dialogues, intended to elicit imaginative thought, Aristotle perfected a careful form of pre-

[1] S. T. Coleridge, *Table Talk*, July 20, 1830, as quoted in H. L. Mencken, *A New Dictionary of Quotations* (New York, Knopf, 1942).

cise lecture, using neat distinctions. The dryness of the result is exaggerated in Aristotle's works as we now have them, since they are largely careful notes on lecture courses, with revisions and additions when a course was repeated or the lecturer changed it.

In one way, therefore, our approach to Aristotle must be quite different from that to Plato. We are not so much concerned with sharing brilliant insights as we are with confronting a detailed, practically argued, common-sense program, grounded in a technical psychology, sociology, epistemology, and cosmology.

Aristotle developed a view of the world in terms of the central ideas of "substance," "cause," "nature," and "power." In the present chapter we will encounter these key ideas as we explore the foundations of his discussion of education.

Before we proceed to a detailed discussion of the nature and function of education in Aristotle's complete philosophy, three preliminary remarks are in order. (1) The first is that we have undertaken, in treating Aristotle, to follow his own rules of method. Thus we will consider briefly the meanings of a few critically important terms that relate Aristotle's philosophy of education to his total philosophy. (2) Next, so much of what is regarded as Aristotelian in modern education is really a transformation of Aristotle's thought that we have documented our presentation heavily in order to permit the reader to think about Aristotle, independently of a tradition bearing his name. (3) Finally, since Aristotle did not write a treatise specifically on education, we must extract his philosophy of education from a large number of works. Commonly, when we want to know what his convictions on education were, we consult a brief passage in the *Politics*, Book viii, which summarizes and discusses briefly the problem of what should be present in a good basic curriculum. However, we will find very little here to explain Aristotle's educational impact on two millennia of Western culture: in law, in science, in politics, in morals, and — indeed — in educational theory proper.

Book viii of the *Politics* can best be regarded as a *doctrine* (not a philosophy) of *basic education* (not of education as a whole). This doctrine of basic education is, moreover, merely developed as a feature of a polity and is accordingly quite narrow. Above all, says Aristotle, the legislator must attend to the education of youth, since, if this is neglected, the constitution suffers.[2] What follows is the outline of the concerns the legislator must have for the fundamental education of the young citizen, as both private citizen and member of the city-state. The welfare of the citizen and that of the city-state are interdependent, and their ends have already been said to be identical.[3] However, such topics as the *nature* of the thing to be educated, the *techniques* of education, the *process* of education, the *function* of education, the *effect* of education, and the *end* of education are hardly discussed at all.

It is the purpose of the present chapter to remove any suspicion that Aristotle's philosophy of education can be fully presented by a reading of *Politics*, Book viii, and to show how Aristotle's educational views are integrally related to the whole of his philosophy.[4]

Aristotle himself indicates that the brief doctrine in the latter part of the *Politics* is embedded in a much larger matrix:

> But since our object is to discover the best form of government, . . . it is evident that we must clearly ascertain the nature of happiness.
>
> We maintain, and have said in the *Ethics*, . . . that happiness is the realization and perfect exercise of virtue. . . . There are three things which make men good and virtuous; these are nature, habit, rational principle. . . . We have already determined what natures are likely to be most easily moulded by the hands of the legislator. *All else* is the work of education; we learn some things by habit and some by instruction.[5]

Thus, even the political context of education points to areas beyond itself. The best form of government is attainable only

[2] *Politics* viii, chap. 1 (1337a10–33). Numbers used in Aristotle citations refer to the pagination of the edition of I. Bekker (Berlin, 1831).
[3] *Ibid.*, Bk. vii, chap. 15 (1337a12–b27).
[4] Surely no one would suppose that Book vii is a *philosophy* of marriage, simply because the legislator's role with respect to marriage is there discussed.
[5] *Politics* vii, chap. 13 (1332a3–1332b11); italics ours. The translation used throughout is that edited by J. A. Smith and W. D. Ross, 13 vols. (Oxford, Oxford University Press, 1908–59).

through knowing what happiness is. Happiness, in turn, is found in the exercise of virtue. And the efficacy of two of the three things essential to virtue, namely, habit and rational principle, depends upon education. "All else," says Aristotle, in summarizing these assertions, "is the work of education." Let us see what is encompassed in this "all else" of habit and rational principle which is the work of education.

II

EUDAIMONIA AND ARETĒ

We must begin with Aristotle's own beginning points, happiness and virtue. The English "happiness" has about it a vague, utilitarian, liberal sound; "virtue" reverberates still with Puritan solemnity. These translations easily lead to important misunderstandings, through sheer anachronism, if for no other reason. The two words which are so translated came into Aristotle's philosophical vocabulary partly, of course, through broad cultural media, but they are also technical terms derivative from the Platonic-Socratic tradition. Much hangs on the meaning of these two terms for Aristotle, and we cannot separate his usage of them from the evolution of meaning which led up to that usage. Firm ground from which to survey Aristotle's philosophy of education thus requires a context even larger than that of his own philosophy.

The Greek word which is translated "happiness" is *eudaimonia*. Another standard rendition is "prosperity." The adjective from the same roots refers to a condition brought about by a good (*eu*) genius or demon (*daimon*). Thus, to the extent that we allow fortune to be personified and to be responsible for all that "happens" (as in our word "happiness"), "good fortune" or "happiness" will serve as fair literary translations. But these are not acceptable philosophically, precisely because they are associated with the idea of an *external* minor deity, a demon, whose favor is gained or received. It is the *externality* of the genius or demon which the main tradition of Greek philosophy rejects. The most conspicuous case is that of Socrates, whose "inner voice" functions as an *internal* spirit. Since the whole of Socrates' life as we know it is colored by his response to this voice, this inner bidding, we should not hesitate to regard it as essential to his very nature, his soul.

Socrates' most famous student, Plato, continues this same notion of *eudaimonia* as depending upon factors largely *internal* to each man. These factors, as internal, are ones which men can, in a proper society, manipulate with at least some success: the love of wisdom, the shaping of one's own soul toward justice, activities of the soul guided by wisdom, etc.[6] Plato's Socrates says flatly that *the whole of one's happiness depends on his education and justice.*[7]

We can thus see a clear line of thought culminating in the acute analysis of Aristotle with regard to *eudaimonia.* The historical Socrates says that no evil can come to a good man either in life or after death.[8] This assertion is a long stride toward internalizing the *daimon* of *eudaimonia;* for what is good is thus not what "happens" to one plainly and simply, but what "happens" from within. Socrates clearly felt that human welfare is largely assignable to the inner factors in men. Plato makes *eudaimonia* a function of the justice and education of the happy man. Aristotle, as we have seen, interprets human "happiness" in terms of virtue, and assigns education a major role in the development of virtue. It will be noticed in passing that these three philosophers, each of whom made a life-long practice of education, in stressing the internality of *eudaimonia,* as opposed to external prosperity or good fortune, were inevitably led to internalize the *daimon,* so that the demon becomes, not a whimsical independent deity dealing blows or blessings to helpless mortals, but an active element in the human soul itself. This internalization of *eudaimonia* was clearly opposed to the conservative theology of the time, and in particular was at odds with the grand fatalism of the tragedians. Both the popular theology and the popular theater had great

[6] *Symposium* 204E ff.; *Gorgias* 470D ff.; *Meno* 88C ff., respectively. Examples of this doctrine abound in Plato; these three citations identify the particular examples given.
[7] *Gorgias* 470E.
[8] *Apology* 41C–D.

use for divine forces that shaped men's lives without regard to
their virtue. Classical Greek philosophy was thus something of
a protest on behalf of humanism. All three philosophers we
have mentioned, of course, made concessions to the fateful or
divine. Socrates started his career in acceptance of the Delphic
Oracle.[9] Plato closes the *Meno* with the ambiguous suggestion
that at least much of virtue is of divine origin, and Aristotle
admits that *eudaimonia* may need some external prosperity,[10]
though elsewhere he speaks of nobility of character as shining
through misfortunes.[11] However, the point to be noticed is
that *education, then as now, is the theory of human effort in
its own behalf, independent of fate or deity.* Conservative
theology regards such theory as impiety; naturalistic philosophy regards it as unscientific.[12]

The other crucial term in Aristotle's philosophy of education is the one usually translated as "virtue." The Greek is
aretē. Here there is less excuse for a stubborn tradition among
translators. Except for a few phrases ("in virtue of," "the
virtue of," etc.) "virtue" connotes for most people "moral
virtue," or often more narrowly, "sexual continence." Thus,
the distinction which Aristotle makes between "intellectual
virtue" and "moral virtue"[13] loses its point. A better translation
is available, one involving fewer risks. "Virtue" means "excellence" or "perfection" of any sort whatever, moral, intellectual, professional, etc. Like *eudaimonia*, it is a mirror word,
its meaning in use being a reflection of the standards of the
time or the author. Thus *aretē* in Homer referred to valor or
prowess.[14] In Plato, *aretē* refers to excellence entire. Plato's
Socrates is strongly opposed to the prevailing common-sense
conviction that a man may have one "virtue" (courage, wis-

[9] *Ibid.*, 20E–21A.

[10] *Nicomachean Ethics* 1099b7–8.

[11] *Ibid.*, 1100b30.

[12] Part of the charge against Socrates was that of impiety. The same
charge was leveled against his philosophical grandson, Aristotle.
(Whereupon Aristotle retired to a private last year of life, lest Athenians "sin twice against philosophy.")

[13] *Ethics* 1103a4 ff.

[14] *Aretē* is cognate to "Arēs," the name of the Greek god of war,
equivalent to the Roman "Mars."

dom, self-control, justice, piety, etc.) without having them all, since all depend on knowledge.[15] It is this factor of *knowledge*, as the underlying condition of "virtue," which Aristotle enlarges upon and treats in a distinctive manner.

Aristotle represents, in his philosophy, the climax of a post-Homeric movement in Greek thought which, by and large, took the major role in human affairs away from the gods and placed it in human hands. The external "demon" becomes an internal "spirit" essential to human existence, but *not* alien to it.[16] Inevitably, with the growth of a doctrine of self-adequacy there appears the growth of a doctrine of self-responsibility. As long as the gods control, then, as far as education goes, men need only learn the arts of war, the traditions of the race, religious and popular mores, domestic skills, etc. But when the heavy responsibility for the course of human affairs is shifted to its human origins, education takes upon itself enormous tasks: psychology (since what men become depends partly upon their self-knowledge), politics, ethics, and social science (for analogous reasons), natural science (since nature now comes to be more and more depersonalized — i.e., ruled not by whim but by regularity), and philosophic education itself become prime necessities for the welfare of the civil polity. And since "virtue" or "excellence" of any kind depends upon knowledge, education not only has a broad subject matter but a central location.

One further point must be made: the new knowledge needed is of a new *kind*. It is not merely authority and tradition ("She died in childbirth because someone in her family had offended Cybele"), nor merely empirical-demonstrative ("To protect your dagger-arm from harm, face the enemy with your sword-arm foremost"). Rather, what is required is the taking of thought, the use of inquiry along lines of rational principle, which tests both the plausibility of tradition and the usability of experience. It is these principles which require further attention.

[15] This is a common theme in Plato; see, for example, *Protagoras* 359 ff.
[16] This internal spirit, or human *daimon*, sets the stage for the later appearance of the Christian "conscience."

III

SCIENCE AND HUMAN NATURE

We begin our investigation of knowledge in a peculiarly pertinent way: Is there such a thing as theoretical knowledge of education — as a discipline, or process — itself? To what extent can we discern the basic principles of education?

On Aristotle's view, we know something when we have demonstrations based on principles which indicate causes.[17] A "principle," *archē*, is a starting point for an inquiry. In studying nature, for example, form, matter, the absence of form ("privation"), and motion are primitive concepts which we can define and discuss but cannot demonstrate: physics is *about* matter, energy, and motion; these properties mark off its proper sphere of discourse, but we do not prove theorems about them in the way we do about falling bodies or specific animals.[18] A body or an animal is a substance which behaves as it does *because* of the laws governing matter in motion. When we can explain this behavior in causal terms, we have genuine knowledge.[19] This is the import of the *Analytics*, in its treatment of scientific knowledge;[20] having read it, we wonder whether we can have this kind of theoretic knowledge of education.

The modern reader must recognize that for Aristotle a "cause" is something that answers the question "Why?" The four "causes" are dimensions of explanation; they are: the *material* cause, the *formal*, the *efficient*, and the *final*. In a house, for example, the material cause is the bricks, lumber, etc., from which the house is made; the formal cause is the structure or blueprint; the efficient cause is the "source of motion," the builder who contributes the energy needed to arrange the materials into a house; the final cause is the purpose served by the house (and it is in terms of *this* purpose or goal that we can best explain *why* a temple, theater, home, and factory differ).[21] Modern thinking has come to equate "cause"

---

[17] *Posterior Analytics* 7167.　　　　　　[18] *Ibid.*, 76b16 ff.
[19] *Ibid.*, 90a5 ff.　　　[20] *Ibid.*, 94a20.　　　　　[21] *Physics* 194b17–195b30.

with only the dimension of efficient causality in Aristotle's scheme.

Book Lambda of the *Metaphysics* opens with the assertion that, in the light of the clarification of the concept of "being" contained in the discussion of Books Alpha through Kappa, we can now see that the causes and principles of all things are the same, though analogically.[22] In other words, the same four dimensions will apply to *any* existent subject matter: but the pattern of four causes must be expected to be relative, in scope and emphasis, to differences in kind.[23] It is proper, then, to expect education to be analyzable in terms of this basic causal scheme, but analyzable in whatever way human actions and learning processes are to be treated.[24]

In the *Physics*, Book II shows the applicability of the four dimensions of causality to natural phenomena and clarifies the general principles used in treating "nature."[25] "Natural philosophy" (which, rather than "physics," is the proper modern translation of Aristotle's science of nature generally) treats of things which contain *within themselves* a principle of change. Change, in turn, involves matter, which, having been without a given form (that is, in a state of "privation"), comes to possess it.[26] For instance, the young animal has certain capacities or potentialities which, if not impeded, will develop in a regular, natural sequence.[27]

---

[22] *Metaphysics* 1071a30.

[23] Technically, analogy holds between things in different genera: cf. *Metaphysics* 1018a13.

[24] *Nicomachean Ethics* 1094b12–1095a10 discusses the method and precision of treatment of such questions.

[25] *Physics* 192b7 ff.

[26] *Ibid.*, 191a3.

[27] The analysis of motion on the level of inorganic substances — what we would think of as "physics" today — worked out rather less satisfactorily within Aristotle's system than the analysis of biological phenomena. The application of the four causes to motion of inorganic substances in the *De Caelo* requires us to think of each kind of element as having a proper place, which it "wants" or "tries" to reach, and to analyze its motion as a whole: the formal cause is not an equation but the path from A (where it starts) to B (its goal, at which it rests). The exception is circular motion. But the theory does not even seem internally consistent: we cannot see, for example, how light from the stars or heat from the sun can be transmitted to the earth on Aristotle's view.

For the purpose of locating educational philosophy in its various dimensions within the Aristotelian system, two doctrines from the works on astronomy and chemistry are peculiarly important. The first is the classification of processes into three kinds: some are cyclical — for example, the revolution of the heavens and the cycle of the seasons; some are epicyclic — for example, the life cycles of different animal species, in which the same sequences repeat, but in different individuals or generations; some are noncyclic or irregularly cyclic, and human history is an example of these.[28] Science in its strict sense is possible for the first two cases, once we recognize the cycle and its period of reiteration; but for the noncyclic process, we cannot have precise prediction or precise demonstration except insofar as there are cycles involved as part of the process in question.[29] In other words, Aristotle's justification of induction in terms of natural cycles and his conviction of human freedom as a cause in history lead him to conclude that *social science, in the sense in which we can have natural science, is impossible.* The second doctrine is that time (which is a numbering of the stages of development or repeated revolutions) is synchronized throughout nature: the energy and disequilibrium responsible for terrestrial process trace back to the different amounts of energy put into the terrestrial region by the sun at different periods, and this regular variation keeps the chronological development sequences of natural substances in synchronization.[30] This suggests a concept of "normal" or "typical" development in biology with a fairly narrow range of individual deviations. But education is concerned with human beings; it is social rather than natural in its affinities, so that a theory of education developed simply by applying scientific method, as we would devise a theory of eclipses, is not possible.

[28] *De Generatione et Corruptione* 337a34–338b20.
[29] *Posterior Analytics* 95a10–96a19: in a system of efficient causality, we can infer antecedent from consequent, but not vice versa unless we are dealing with a cycle. The fact that human agency is indeterminate ("free") is a metaphysical fact, discussed in *Metaphysics* 1046a37–b28.
[30] *De Generatione et Corruptione* 336b12–337a33.

IV

Human Nature: Sense, Habit, and Reason

We have seen that man's happiness lies largely in his own hands, and that indeed the very word which is translated as "happiness" means essentially "perfection" (*eu* as in "eugenics") of "spirit" (*daimon*). Moreover, the methods which science employs — those, in fact, which presume that its objects are automata — are limited in their applicability to human affairs. Education in the broad sense of cultivation (*paideia*) will have as its task, then, the perfection of human potentialities along lines which will submit to group procedures but will necessarily, in fine grain, include a calculus of individual differences as well. Aristotle himself repeatedly draws this conclusion with respect to the moral virtues.[31] Nonetheless, certain general principles of human nature and human behavior are discernible. These general principles will throw light on the problems of education as a whole, as well as serving to elaborate Aristotle's somewhat cryptic coupling of education and the best form of government.

Indeed, human nature and conduct might be said to be the main emphases of the *De Anima* and the *Nichomachean Ethics*, respectively, although there is considerable overlap. It is in the *De Anima* that we find the classical — and by now nearly vacuous — construing of man as a rational animal.[32] This formula in its context is by no means empty, however, nor is it so simple as it seems.

With the animals man shares the functions of nutrition, locomotion, reproduction, and respiration. With the more complex animals man shares sense, imagination, pleasure and pain, and the capacity for habit formation.[33] If we substitute for the four-element chemistry of Aristotle the modern conception of ninety-two "natural" elements, we can construct from the

[31] E.g., *Ethics* 1105a32 ff.; 1115b7.
[32] *De Anima* 414a4–27.
[33] *Ethics* 1179b33 ff. shows the relation of habit to character. A particularly clear and interesting statement of the role of "custom" in the association of ideas is given in *De Memoria* 452a26.

Parva Naturalia a remarkable counterpart of modern behavior-ism.[34] In *De Motu* (which, however, may not be authentic), the behavioristic treatment is particularly marked.[35] Unlike the social insects, which seemed channeled by nature into one unique set of habits (Aristotle suggests it may be because they lack the capacity of using language), men are conditioned environmentally in the most divergent ways. The nonrational, i.e., the animal part, of man is partly within his control, partly not. There is even a sense, then, in which part of his animality can be said to be rational — in that it will submit to rational control ("having a tendency to obey as one does one's father"), and indeed the continent or temperate man is one whose appetitive faculties lie under rational restriction.[36] The crucial point is this: *Man as animal has a natural capacity for habit formation, but there is no necessity that he form one rather than another complete set of habits.* Aristotle plainly thinks that by taking thought men can add to their stature.

We are thus led to the consideration of the other aspect of human nature, its rationality. We begin with the basic link between man's animal nature and his rational nature: sensation. Men have sensations, resulting from the efficient causal action

[34] The notion that all natural things are reducible to "earth, water, air, and fire" seems to our modern view a fancy so childishly simple as to be beyond defense. Yet if we regard these as generic names of *states* of matter, they adapt rather well to our conceptions of solid, liquid, gaseous, and free energy respectively. Greek insight often outran Greek vocabulary, and the more or less conscious metaphysical extension of terms was common. For instance, Aristotle's Greek had no term for sheer matter as such; so he employed the Greek word for "lumber" (*hylē*). No one would suppose that he therefore held to the doctrine that everything which occupied space was composed of lumber. We ourselves use the same metaphysical extension, partly by tradition, partly for convenience. We speak of the "rare earths," hydraulic brakes (usually oil-operated), and hydrodynamics (the dynamics of fluid states); and lately "fluid states" have been treated to include gases as special instances.

[35] Cf., for example, *De Motu* 701b1 ff.: "The movements of animals may be compared with those of automatic puppets. . . ." But authentic or not, there seems nothing here inconsistent with the first chapter of the authentic *De Partibus Animalium.* We should note in passing that *ideas* rank among the *stimuli* in this Aristotelian arc. The *De Motu* passage with the translator's notes in the Oxford translation is worth further study by anyone interested in the history of learning theory.

[36] *Ethics* 1102b12–1103a14.

of sensible properties of objects on their senses.[37] The content of all our knowledge and the impetus to use our faculties always originate in sense perception. But the reports of the separate senses are combined, and the properties of number, figure, motion, and shape are recognized, by the "common sense."[38] Sensory images, or phantasms, are recalled by memory in accordance with definite laws of association, and such images always accompany more abstract thought.[39] Memory naturally associates images which are similar, or which are close in space and time in our experience; through learning, other habits of association can be developed, of which that of causal connection is the most important.[40] However, certain skills cannot be taught, but only guided. For example, that "genius" which is the native talent for discerning aesthetic likenesses and differences, and which cannot be taught, seems to be a sensitivity of imagination.[41] On the other hand, the art of mnemonics, by which some standard learned pattern is used to frame or correlate with a list to be remembered, is a special case of developing habits of association in the memory.[42]

Beyond memory and imagination, as we move more solidly into the area of the specifically human, man has the capacities of abstraction, discursive thinking, and intellectual intuition.[43] If it is true that we would not think at all without sense experience as impetus and matter for thought, it is equally true, in

[37] *De Anima* II, chaps 5–12 (416b31–424b19).

[38] For the necessity of sensation, cf., for example, *De Anima* 432a7. The "common sense" is treated in *ibid.*, 424b20–427a15.

[39] *Ibid.*, 432a8; cf. *De Memoria* 450a ff.

[40] *De Memoria* 451b23: "Such is the empirical ground of the process of recollection; for the mnemonic movements . . . are in some cases identical, in others, again, simultaneous, with those of the idea we seek. . . ." Association by causality is treated under scientific inquiry, but at 452a3 memory of causal sequences (well-ordered, like the successive demonstrations in geometry) is treated. Such well-ordering makes recollection peculiarly easy. The principle of association by similarity-opposition-contiguity is an anticipation of Hume.

[41] *Poetics* 1459a5; compare the statement about the special sensitivity required for the most accurate interpretation of dreams, *On Prophecy in Sleep* 464b7 ff.

[42] *De Memoria* 451a12–15, and the exception at 451b14. Hippias the Sophist had developed an "art of memory," as Socrates mentions twice in Plato's *Hippias Minor*.

[43] *De Anima* 429b18; *Ethics* 1139b20–35.

Aristotelian psychology, that an innate desire to know leads us to recognize in this sensuous manifold the structures, systematic interconnections, and teleological organization in things. (1) Abstraction is the faculty of regarding structures as if they existed separately; mathematics, and recognition of formal causes so far as these are revealed in *schemata*, are closely connected with this faculty.[44] (2) Discursive thinking leads us to order concepts and experiences into systems, of the sort we have seen in our previous discussion of the nature of scientific demonstration. (3) Intellectual intuition is the faculty which grasps principles: basic classifications and axioms that cannot be demonstrated.[45] It is also involved in concept formation, when we recognize a definition as correctly stating "what it is to be" this or that. To know what it is to be something, we must be able to see in that thing its final cause — the goal which emerges from its successive structural modifications.

The topic of final cause deserves special attention. We recall that for Aristotle knowledge is a knowledge of causes, among which is the final cause — the "that for the sake of which the thing has become as it has." In modern thought the functional explanation of artifacts is taken for granted; we would not think of *explaining* a piece of machinery without explaining what the parts are "for." Also, functional explanation is common in the accounts of living things, insofar as we are concerned with *organization of subordinate parts;* e.g., "The ink sac of the squid is for protection." But when we come to ask what squids themselves are "for" — or what men are "for" — we are embarrased by a hoary theology and related doctrines which suppose that such questions can be answered only in terms of a divine architect or a conscious creator. Aristotle was not hampered by these considerations, nor was he confronted by a doctrine of evolution. For Aristotle, an efficient cause and the substance of which it is the cause *must be in the same species.*[46] There is thus no origin of species, but rather an

---

[44] *Metaphysics* 1026a7, 1078a7. See on this point R. Brumbaugh, "Aristotle as a Mathematician," *Review of Metaphysics*, Vol. VIII, No. 3 (March, 1955). Cf. *Ethics* 1142a18; *De Anima* 431b13.

[45] *Ethics* 1140b31–1141a7; *Posterior Analytics* 100b10–17.

[46] *Metaphysics* 1033b29–1034a8.

eternity of species. As eternal, man has a place in nature, and therefore a definite role or function. The specifically human function, the reason why he exists, what he is "for," is the development of his rationality, both in practical and in intellectual affairs. Rationality is not merely the distinguishing feature of humanity; it is the best. "If happiness [*eudaimonia*, here in the sense of well-being] is activity in accordance with virtue [*aretē*, excellence], it is reasonable that it should be in accordance with the highest virtue, and this will be the excellence of the best part of us."[47] Aristotle makes out an extremely good case for the rational element as the best element. Indeed, that is the major import of Book x of the *Nichomachean Ethics*. Pleasure is shared with animals,[48] and amusement is shared with children.[49] But the crucial weakness of all other forms of human pursuit, insofar as they are thought to contribute to that perfection of spirit which is what Aristotle's "happiness" means etymologically, is that they are too subject to the whims of fortune: this is true of wealth, fame, power, etc., any of which may be laudable, but all are insecure. The man whose "happiness" rests in the active cultivation of his rationality owns and guides himself in a way that those who identify their lives with events subject to external fortune do not. This notion is the direct descendant of Socrates' injunction "Know Thyself," and his conviction that the *daimon* of *eudaimonia* is internal to man, not external to him.

We saw above that the part of the rational faculty which grasps the essential character of things, including what they are "for," is the "intellectual intuition." The most significant thing in this psychology is the partial autonomy and mutual dependence of these faculties: the higher cannot operate without the lower to provide them with material and energy; the lower without the higher are devoid of control and specific direction, and habit plus memory provides their only order, as we see in other animals than man.

Only at the end of the *De Anima* does Aristotle indicate that his treatment of reason has been largely oriented toward theoretic thinking, and that if we introduce pleasure and pain, and a social context with attendant friendships and demands of

[47] *Ethics* 1177a11 ff.   [48] *Ibid.*, 1118a23 ff.   [49] *Ibid.*, 1176b32 ff.

citizenship, another dimension is needed in this already fairly complex account of human thought.[50]

V

MORAL EDUCATION AND SELF-REALIZATION

In the *Nichomachean Ethics*, in the context of the problem of full individual self-realization, this other dimension is supplied. Ethics is a practical, *not* a theoretical, science; so it must proceed by combining, clarifying, and rendering consistent common opinion and that of experts, to come to those of its principles which cannot be supplied by special study.[51] However, we do know that human nature includes a capacity for habit formation on the level of appetite and passion. It includes, moreover, a latent "desire to know," expressed as an inveterate (though often undirected or fruitless) curiosity. Thirdly, there is a natural final cause for man — the kind of dignified complete development which we would design as the outcome of a plan for the noblest or most admirable sort of person. These three principles do not preclude cultural relativity, of course. Any modern reader of the *Ethics*, for example, would consider some habits which would be included as admirable by an Athenian of Aristotle's time reprehensible in our own culture, close as it is to the former.[52] On the other hand, when we consider control of appetite and passion, in an effort to define "moral virtue," we may fairly use contemporary cultural expressions of praise and blame. These indicate where, within the social framework, we recognize dimly something admirable or the reverse in other men.[53] An important point about the

[50] *De Anima* 431a15–433b30.

[51] *Ethics* 1140a25–30; 1094b12–1095a12.

[52] For instance, the "greatness of soul" which appears as a virtue at 1123a32 (translated as "pride" in the Oxford edition) provoked a Scotch commentator to remark that "no man of sensibility can resist an urge to kick Aristotle's *ho megalopsuchos*." The details of the stereotype picture of this "proud" man — slow gait, deep voice, level speech, preferring to remember favors he has done rather than those he has received, a collector of beautiful and useless things, etc. — give an interesting insight into the way that excellence may be expressed in a culture.

[53] This interrelation is developed in Books iii through v.

admiration which leads to praise is that it is a partial recognition of the natural final cause of man, as realized in the person we admire.

Aristotle holds that excellence of moral character lies somewhere in a mean between extremes of repression and uninhibited expression of all passions and appetites.[54] In doing so he may have unwittingly given us a definition of civilization, regardless of its particular patterns of expression and repression. Such habits of moderation are learned by taking deliberate action of a moderate sort; mere lectures on the theory of morals will not of themselves have any effect on moral character.[55] On the other hand, habits may be formed by a course of action based on a reasoned desire for self-improvement; the individual is not helpless in the face of his family or his community as conditioning agencies.[56] Where he is helpless — and one reason for the elaborate tracing of philosophic context is that it seems needed to give Aristotle's exact meaning on this point — is in any hope for magic. Neither reasoning nor wishing, but only repeated deliberate action becoming habitual, will change a man's character.[57] And without self-realization in this domain, happiness is beyond a man's grasp. Classroom instruction can thus contribute little to the *moral* education which makes other education possible. But this is not a naturalistic or relativistic analysis. It is true that the imagining of ourselves in the places of our fellow citizens is accompanied by pleasure or pain, and this fact depends partly on what other people say about us; still, pure reason is at work, at least as a goal, insofar as our admiration and pleasure reflect a felt tendency toward natural final causality. Further, in all practical decisions, experience, prudence, and science are needed to avoid choosing means which will destroy or fail to achieve our proper ends.[58]

The consideration of objectivity in our dealing with other men, which results from the recognition that they are like ourselves, and the habit of fairness in our dealings with them, is the

[54] The definition in *Ethics* ii, chaps. 5–7 (1105b17–1108b10), is not qualified by reference to any specific culture, and probably need not be.
[55] *Ethics* 1094b27 ff., and the much stronger statement, 1105b13.
[56] *Ibid.*, 1104b17; 1144b1–1145a10.
[57] *Ibid.*, 1104b17.
[58] *Ibid.*, 1141b2–1143a18.

transition, in the *Ethics*, from moral to intellectual excellence.[59] In the moral virtues, the rule of "nothing too much" is the base conception. But this traditional notion of the fundamental principle of the gentleman's code emphatically does not apply with respect to intellectual virtue. However, just as man has an extraordinary range of possible customs and moral habits, so he has a wide spectrum of directions and kinds of intellectual development.[60] Arts and skills, prudence, facility with abstractions, good memory, clear intuition, knowledge of science, are among the distinct intellectual excellences discussed here; they are not interchangeable, not all learned in the same way; not all men have equal aptitude for all of them. Neither is there any single ideal pattern which we can set down as giving each individual person the greatest happiness of which he is by nature capable.[61] Each of these capacities must be developed in its own proper way, with proper materials; we have already seen, for example, that practical sciences are different in kind from theoretical ones.[62]

In all these intellectual activities, though, there is a common element: active mind, giving direction and an operative (though not necessarily fully realized) goal present throughout the processes of perceiving and cognizing, abstracting and evaluating. When we can exhibit this goal as realized in its purest form, in theoretic contemplation, we have related the theory of human nature and conduct to a proper and natural common final cause for man. Man is bound both by his animal nature and by his desire to realize his distinctive rationality. Such realization takes many patterns and paths, depending on aptitudes, culture, and education.[63] However, this final pointing to the ideal of maximum realization of rationality, in *Ethics* x, simply supplements the discussion of Book vi by pointing out the final cause as a common denominator of the forms that full

---

[59] *Ibid.*, Bk. v (1129 ff.).

[60] Thus *Ethics* vi considers science, art, practical wisdom, intuitive reason, philosophic wisdom, political science, skill in deliberation, understanding, and judgment severally.

[61] *Ethics* 1144b1 ff.: but there *is* a common *goal*. *Ibid.*, 1144b30 ff.; 1174b10, 1175b1.

[62] See also *ibid.*, 1143b17–1144a35.

[63] *Ibid.*, 1179a32 ff.

intellectual self-development of an individual may take.[64] Given suitable moral character, the individual's own pleasure and pain in learning will be a good guide to his full intellectual realization, since those activities for which he has talent will be most pleasant to him. We must depend upon his prudence to prevent him from specializing too exclusively in these, to the detriment of his proper physical and psychological balance.

VI

THE CURRICULUM

Before we return to the estimation of those actual curricular convictions which Aristotle supports in the *Politics* and elsewhere, it may be useful to summarize the main features of the philosophical matrix in which the theory of education is embedded.

Education, for Aristotle, is education toward an end: the perfection of human nature. The well-being of men consists in the *activity* of perfection. It follows that education is a lifelong process. "Education" has as its root meaning the idea of "leading out," as in the Latin word *e-ducere*.[65] The problems of education are the problems of leading out, that is, of developing the unique and best part of human nature, in company with those features of life which it shares with other living beings. What is brought to perfection is latently present in men as potentiality. The good life is one in which the potentialities are brought to fullest fruition. The importance of the task of education, not as a mere perpetuator of tradition, nor as a mere practical expedient, but as training in the art of inquiry, looms larger as men come to realize how extensively

[64] *Ibid.*, 1174b22 ff.

[65] The actual derivation is not direct. "Education" comes from *educatus*, the past participle of *educare*, "to rear" or "to nourish." Some authorities prefer to say that *educere*, "to educate," and *educare* are "related" and nothing more. However, the Merriam-Webster *Third New International Dictionary* gives the account of *educare* as *e-ducare* (from *ducere*). Moreover, the definitive *Thesaurus Linguae Latinae* (Leipzig, 1904–1942), lists "to educate" among the meanings for both words.

their future can be shaped by their own deliberation and action.

Education has general principles. These are the principles which take account of the general features of human nature. Crucial to the conception of human nature is the concept of its having a natural goal, given incipiently, as the oak is incipiently in the acorn, the goal being that of rational perfection, both in realms of intellect and in areas of practice. These ends serve those of the good city-state and vice versa. Albeit education is a social science, one which deals with the various in human nature as well as the regular. It can never rely upon generalities to work universally without modification.

Lastly, just as active intellect cannot function without the largely automatic action of the senses which provide it with data for discernment, ordering, and analysis, so also the habits which underlie the good life in its manifold aspects, whether in practical or theoretical affairs, can be acquired only through actual habituation. *Mere thought, desire, resolution, etc., are powerless against the crushing weight of the repeated act — the reinforced pattern of action which arises from it.*

We may now fairly return to the point at which the study began: the curriculum in civil polity (which is a more instructive and less misleading translation of *politeia* than "politics"). It is clear that both moral character and a beginning of intellectual development depend upon the family and the community. The laws of the latter Aristotle explicitly recognizes as an educative agency.[66] The individual can in fact attain self-realization only in society and thus is by nature (insofar as his final cause determines this nature) a "political animal."[67] Almost every question that occurs to a modern educator reading *Politics* viii falls in some other discipline than political science as Aristotle conceived and delimited it. Operating "dialectically," in terms of expert and general opinion, he was able to summarize the aims of education in three categories that still hold: (1) some want it to be useful to the individual economically, (2) some want it to be training for good citizenship, (3) some want it to be "liberal," that is, planned with a

[66] *Ethics* 1179a30–end.
[67] *Politics* 1253a20–37.

view to preparation for "the higher learning."[68] Without leaving the realm of practical political discussion, Aristotle found himself able to propose a curriculum which would satisfy all three objectives.

Children should be taught, in a system of compulsory public education, gymnastic, reading and writing (using classical literature in the reading course), reckoning, drawing and music (including technical training in musical performance, though not technical in the way in which we would teach technique to a professional performer). This seems a far cry from the array of disciplines: biology, psychology, metaphysics, ethics, and logic, at Aristotle's disposal — until we notice that this blandly offered practical suggestion is in fact capable of being defended in depth and buttressed by considerations from every other aspect of Aristotle's system of philosophy. The offhand "compromise" begins to look (as we would expect of the educational proposals by any of Plato's students) like a program with an elaborate, though not explicit, philosophic rationale.

The one place where Aristotle does to some extent show his hand in *Politics* viii itself is in answering an anticipated objection (from all three standpoints) that it is foolish to spend public funds on music lessons involving student performance. One might defend music appreciation as liberal education or even as good training for a citizen, who will be participating in decisions about the fine arts, but why lessons in technique? The justification is double: it is impossible to have full appreciation of any art or craft unless one has had firsthand technical experience in it, and participation in musical activity is a worthwhile use of leisure, one which we expect our students to continue, even in old age.[69] The first point should be noted carefully by educators who suppose there is a polar opposition between Aristotle and Dewey. From the very nature of "art," it follows that we are dealing with a way of *purposive ordering of a medium*, that is, we are dealing with materials (this is especially obvious in the plastic arts) which have latent possi-

[68] *Ibid.*, 1337a41; the whole of viii, chap. 2, balances these proposed aims of education, with concessions to each.

[69] *Ibid.*, chaps. 5–7 (1339a12–end).

bilities of organization toward some end. The end and the agency which develops it are, of course, external to the material, rather than internal to it, as in the case of a living being. Through practice we come to recognize the potentialities that technique can elicit. To "appreciate" art is to some extent dependent on a creative insight into it; on this level, at least, "active mind" knows by "making."[70] The same principle applies to both fine and useful arts, and even to pure mathematics regarded aesthetically.[71] The second point follows from the double conception of happiness and the end of man which is developed in other contexts. Happiness is a kind of self-realization — that is, it is an *activity*;[72] but the most self-rewarding and intrinsically pleasant activities of man are those of intellectual inquiry and aesthetic activity.[73] The standard way of teaching literature in Aristotle's time included first-hand participation in dramatic acting, so that no separate justification of this was required. Learning by doing was old when Rome was a town.

In the *Politics* Aristotle's defense of drawing is that it is instrumental, as an aid not in business transactions, but in judging architecture and sculpture.[74] But the strongest justification for the casual inclusion of drawing here lies in the role of the *schema* in the *De Anima*.[75] To observe accurately requires attention to the "common sensibles" which coordinate and give a frame of structure for the qualities of pure sensation. To connect experience with abstract concepts (which we always think of as accompanied by an imagined instance or image) we must have a *schematism* in the imagination, that is, the capacity to convert abstract mathematical concepts into visual representation. Attention to number, figure, and magnitude is the proper concern of the "common sense." A specific teaching of such attention, with the motor habits involved in

[70] *Ibid.*, 1340b20–33. At b23 Aristotle remarks: "It is difficult, if not impossible, for those who do not perform to be good judges of the performance of others."

[71] So, at least, we would interpret the discussion of "art" in *Ethics* vi, and the treatment of mathematics and the beautiful in *Metaphysics* M 3.

[72] *Ethics* 1098a16 ff., 1099b25 ff.

[73] *Metaphysics* 980a1; *Poetics* 1447a9.

[74] *Politics* 1338a35 ff.

[75] *De Anima* 430a17; cf. *De Memoria* 450a1 ff.

reproduction of the structures underlying sensation, is a training of the mind to habits of discrimination and attention. Whether this will "transfer" depends, of course, on whether the subject is taught with a proper view to the three objectives set down: practical utility, usefulness for citizenship, and suitable preparation for higher learning. It is when we think of both a general principle and a type case that we are really thinking most precisely; the ability to see the type case clearly is a property of memory and imagination.[76] It would be a bit over-mathematical and would neglect motion if the drawing course did not take account of the dynamic structures presented in nature, art, and literature; but Aristotle's statement in the *Poetics* that he thinks of the object of imitation of the painter as *character* suggests that the drawing course will take cognizance of various nonpictorial dynamic dimensions (as it must if it is to imitate "nature," which, we note from the *Physics* and the *Ethics*, is basically dynamic).[77]

Calculation is taught less as an end in itself and more as a needed skill: it seems that this work is less a foretaste, for the pupil, of a self-rewarding activity suitable to a happy life than music and drawing are.[78] But the justifications are not limited to the usefulness of calculation for business, household management, political decision, and the study of pure mathematics.[79] All discursive thinking, whether theoretic or practical, proceeds by sequential linking operations which are sometimes described as "calculative" by Aristotle.[80] The operations of computation are an anticipation, as close as an elementary pupil's capacities will anticipate them, of basic forms and operations of discursive thought. The joint demands of advocates of utility, social value, and liberal education seem

[76] *Metaphysics* M 1087a5–25.

[77] *Poetics* 1448a5–7; cf. *Physics* ii, 1a2b7 ff.

[78] *Politics* 1338a36.

[79] Aristotle seems quite ready to admit that mathematics has a certain beauty, and even that the forms of beauty are analyzed by applying concepts (e.g., magnitude, order) that are mathematical. He does not, however, endorse Plato's notion that mathematics is "charming," and has not left any systematic work on pure mathematics.

[80] So, at the end of *Prior Analytics* ii, chapters 22 to 27 (67b26 ff.) show that comparisons of value, persuasion, induction, etc., are all like the syllogism formally.

essential to insure that a sufficient range of typical "calculation" situations will be used in teaching to safeguard against the danger of presenting merely abstract forms, not related through experience and habit to relevant sorts of content.

Reading and writing involve considerable drill, but the reading will include classical literature. Presumably writing and spelling will include copying down literary passages from dictation. The reading will include dramatic recitation by the students. It is probably here that the state will want to exercise most supervision over choice of school materials, for civics and ethics will be learned in connection with this literary study, in the only way an elementary student can begin to learn them. This is by "example" and "fable," to take two technical terms from the *Rhetoric*, the latter of which is like (though lacking in the validity of) scientific induction.[81]

There is thus a provision in this curriculum for the acquisition of skills which will *continue* to be of value throughout life, and which will specifically develop, by practical exercises forming sound habits, capacities of aesthetic expression, close observation and clear imagination, accuracy in discursive "calculation," and acquaintance through literary examples with concepts of citizenship and admirable character.

Beyond this point, we may expect a pupil in Aristotle's envisaged culture to be self-propelling in his desire for further education, along lines of his special aptitude and interest particularly, but with a realization in mind, based on experience, that happiness lies in the fullest intellectual and moral self-expression and self-development.

The social effect of this sound basis and impetus given to man's natural capacities in the educational scheme should be what Plato had envisaged in Book v of the *Republic*: if any state improves its education, its institutions will be improved automatically.[82] Aristotle, in the educational program in his political treatise, does not dwell on the schools as an instrument

[81] *Rhetoric* 1356b1 ff.

[82] *Politics* ii, in which Aristotle examines proposed utopias, notes that these thinkers think of social change and social forces almost exclusively in terms of education. Cf. Plato, *Republic* v, 424A; this passage and its context are discussed in Brumbaugh, *Plato's Mathematical Imagination*, pp. 87 ff.

for advocating revolution or as an agency for social improvement.[83] But it does follow that the political desire to improve a constitution that is not ideal will be stronger and more effective as the citizens recognize what the individual man can hope to develop into, given a community where the good man and the good citizen are the same.[84] In the complex of political causes, the efficient cause of revolutionary potential develops as the discrepancy between good citizenship and ideal individual development is realized by the citizen, who sees that the two final causes should be, but are not, the same. However the state may select materials with a view to its self-preservation, a sound basic program of public education will, if Aristotle is right in his philosophy, lead to progressive improvement and change, to gradual "revolution."

VII

Conclusion

The conclusion we suggest is that Aristotle's work is capable of providing us with a rather full philosophy of education when we read that work in the context of his total philosophy.[85] A further specific point emerges. There seems no real quarrel between Aristotle's notion of education as disciplined cultivation of the intellect and Dewey's notion of education as development of skills through motivated experience, on the level of elementary education. At a higher level, Aristotle would probably contend that new development of rational capacity makes possible a kind of theoretic inquiry

[83] In fact, he points out that the state will supervise and exercise censorship over the public educational system.

[84] *Politics* v, Chapter 1 (1301a20–1302a17), introduces the treatment of social forces and social change with the generalization that ordinary states are based on incorrect ideas of justice, and this situation leads to discontent and revolution.

[85] In making this point, we have stressed the principles in philosophical context relevant to understanding *Politics* viii, rather than the detailed explication of that book itself; such a detailed commentary in the context here sketched in is also necessary for the reconstruction of Aristotle's philosophy of education.

which Dewey might consider of doubtful value. But if we cannot appreciate music without experience in making it, and if we must select specific types of training for each of the psychological capacities that we hope to develop, while recognizing that intellectual excellence can take many forms, we should, as Aristotelians, have little quarrel with modern progressive education.

Aristotle could write that "all men by nature desire to know," yet admit learning is sometimes a painful process.[86] He could hope to induce students to undergo the work of learning for the sake of gratification of their impulse to grow psychologically. Critical of the Platonic Academy, because of its stress on mathematics as giving the forms of thought (without, Aristotle thought, an equally needed attention to content), and because of its assumption that dialectic could teach students how to apply these forms universally, Aristotle projected an alternative view of education.

Ironically, his authority has been cited to justify notions he would certainly not have approved. The trivium and quadrivium, which repeat the Platonic optimism in their stress on form, are examples. So are interpretations of his program of elementary education as a recognition that we need intellectual discipline, learning by routine, on this level, with applications and enjoyment of the work deferred until the student becomes adult. Such accentuation of the painful element present in the learning process would be the surest way to turn men into haters of discourse and learning; for faulty conditioning can abort those sequential stages of development which, under other conditions, emerge as the admirable if complex harmony of faculties that is "human nature."

In this balanced classical view of human excellence and its realization, Aristotle introduces important doctrines and assumptions that later developments of science, society, and educational experience lead us to question. We will encounter these criticisms of Aristotelian ideas as we look at four later philsophers, two in the eighteenth and two in the twentieth century, who make significant contributions to the philosophy of education.

[86] *Politics* 1340b15; *Ethics* 1175a3; *Metaphysics* 1074b27.

Suggestions for Further Reading

Aristotle, unlike Plato, is not an easy philosopher to read and appreciate. His tremendous range of interests and his judicious attention to the four "causal dimensions" of each area he discusses have led to many interpretations, each of which singles out one perspective for emphasis. Perhaps the best approach is to begin by way of the ideas of "cause," "substance," and "nature," key ideas around which analyses are organized. R. McKeon's Introduction to *The Basic Works of Aristotle* (New York, Random House, 1947) is a good, if somewhat tightly written, discussion of this approach. The works of Aristotle have been translated into English in thirteen volumes, under the editorship of J. A. Smith and W. D. Ross (Oxford, Oxford University Press, 1908–59). A survey of the contents of these volumes, ranging from logic to fragments of early dialogues, will give the student an appreciation of the enormous mastery and range of subject matter that Aristotle had at his disposal, organized into separate specialized systematic treatises. Education, as we have indicated, is too complex to fall into any single natural classification; the *Politics* and *Nicomachean Ethics*, dealing with social organization and individual self-realization, respectively, are the most interesting and relevant treatises, and it is here one should begin. But there remain connections to be followed in the light of one's particular interest. We have indicated some of these in the footnotes to the present chapter.

Among secondary sources, we mention three: A. E. Taylor, *Aristotle* (London, Nelson, 1943), W. D. Ross, *Aristotle* (London, Methuen, 1937), and J. H. Randall, Jr., *Aristotle* (New York, Columbia University Press, 1960).

CHAPTER FOUR

Rousseau: Émile, *A Romance of Education*

I

THE IDEA OF NATURAL GROWTH

At first glance, Rousseau's romantic praise of nature is anachronistic in the twentieth century. The idea of the noble savage has been obliterated by practical field work in anthropology. The rural life breeds undesirable citizens (like Jeeter Lester in *Tobacco Road*) as readily as do the slums of great cities. Moreover, Rousseau's florid, emotional style seems unrealistic to the modern reader. Nevertheless, Rousseau's *Émile* continues to find sympathetic readers, partly because some of its ideas belong to our own body of common sense today and partly because the rambling disquisition has a cumulative power which cannot be stated in abstract paraphrase.

Rousseau's idea of nature continues a theme which we found important in classical discussion. In general it seems Aristotelian in its presuppositions.[1] It modifies Aristotle's view, however, in several important respects. For Aristotle, human nature is defined by a goal or "final cause," the complete self-realization of an admirable adult. This adult capability is

[1] See Chapter Three, especially Section VI.

76

"potentially" in the growing child, and growth and skill must be attained by sequential stages: direction must be preserved, and no step left out, when we consider education as growth toward self-realization.[2] But just here is trouble for the pupil, if not for the theorist, for the "child as potential adult" view would deny that childhood as such has any final cause of its own, apart from that of preparation for a later career. Rousseau totally opposed the Aristotelian theory of his time by arguing that the child at each age has an actually attained nature, and therefore a proper final cause of his own. Childhood is not, then, a state of privation to be got through and transformed by adding increments of adult skill and perfection, but is a state of a living organism that can have intrinsic value in itself, as long as the "nature" of the child is recognized and respected. On this point, Rousseau's new insight has become important and widely accepted in educational theory; we will encounter the non-Aristotelian view of nature that he proposed in the otherwise very diverse thought of Kant, of Dewey, and of Whitehead. A further modification made by Rousseau, or at least a new emphasis introduced by him on a point where Aristotle is noncommittal, is his observation that the rate of growth of a human being is explicitly discontinuous; there are long plateaus and sudden spurts, marked by rapid change of natural impulses and interests, as the child progresses normally from infancy to adulthood. It will not do, then, to be content with steady progress on a smooth curve. The learner is not naturally growing in that rather stolid way, and his training and lessons cannot be programmed (with or without a teaching machine) so smoothly, either.

For Rousseau, here again departing radically in emphasis at least from Aristotle, the great danger in child raising, as in gardening, is environmental. Weeds choking the soil, or the gardener's ill-considered urge to "force" the crop can ruin the natural growth of the young mind. Children form habits from their contacts, and these habits will be formed as society conditions them — so far Aristotle and Rousseau agree. But

[2] This end-directed characteristic of *all* "nature" (See Aristotle, *Physics* i, ii) carries over to Aristotle's treatment of *human* nature in the practical sciences.

Rousseau believes that all society rests on an unnatural inequality of power and status which denies and destroys the natural equality and dignity of man. The child in "society" is first forced into a role of unhealthful docility, then taught a set of values that presuppose one man's being able to master the will of another. In Rousseau's view, all this is an inversion of nature by society. A child, to develop naturally, must therefore be insulated from society, at least society in its modern, and particularly in its urban, form. It is instructive to contrast this conclusion with that of Aristotle, for whom man is by nature a "political animal"; only his participation in society can create the "second nature" by which he becomes truly human.

Rousseau even extends his dour view of society's effects into his reflections on botany: Cultivated fruit trees, he writes, are stunted and deformed, compared to those in nature unaffected by contact with human societies. Perhaps, he hopes, the example of a single test case can show well enough what human nature can be, cultivated by a skillful gardener who removes weeds of precocity and perversity from the environment, to tempt society at large toward educational reforms. At any rate, Émile presents itself as such a case study.[3]

From the educator's point of view, one of the worst features of society is the premium it puts on forced precocity. The child is always being taught skills and given ideas which he cannot understand or see the use of. He should not be persuaded by praise, or even by pleasure, to invest time and attention in mastery of symbols with referents quite beyond his concrete experience, or in skills for which his nature at a given stage is not ready. This is a principle with which we will find John Dewey agreeing enthusiastically; but in his detailed application of it, Dewey has a much more liberal and more socially oriented conception of what is "meaningful" than is apparent in the nonsocial psychology of Rousseau. We will see, in the story of Émile, that one of the most critical dangers confronting the boy and his tutor, Jean Jacques, is the latter's constant temptation to anticipate nature via pedagogical

[3] Our citations of Émile will be from the Everyman edition (trans. Barbara Foxley, with introduction by A. B. DeMonvel, New York, Dutton, 1911).

art, academic discipline, or moral disquisition. The good tutor's self-restraint in this matter is assisted by his recollection of various case studies among the children of wealthy families he has known. Émile is not taught to read, for example, until he suddenly wants to, when, at twelve to fifteen, he is "ready" and easily masters a skill that would have required infinite discipline, disinterest, and time had he been "taught" in the usual manner from the age of four.[4] Analogously, according to Rousseau, a child may enjoy parallel play with other children but is really incapable of enforced socialization until his nature has become that of a youth or man.

The modern reader may begin to see why Rousseau's ideas have a good deal of contemporary interest. For example, there are our competing modern theories: one advocates the learning of skills early, the other recommends waiting for readiness while concentrating on socialization. But if Rousseau is right, both of these theories are wrong.[5]

It is not, however, until we recognize that philosophies may, and in fact must, sometimes be expressed through a literary rather than an abstract discursive form — a lesson our modern existentialists are teaching — that we are able to see why *Émile* gives the feeling of unity it does, while an abstract summary of its "argument" is either incoherent or hopelessly incomplete. It is generally true of Rousseau's work that his treatments of the themes of nature, society, and education

[4] An interesting educational experiment, in which children are allowed to develop and learn without discipline, in terms of their own readiness, has been conducted at an English school (see A. S. Neill, *Summerhill: A Radical Approach to Child Rearing*, New York, Hart, 1960). American interest in the Summerhill program has led to the establishment of the Summerhill Society in New York and the publication of the *Summerhill Bulletin*. An article in the first issue describes recent conventional studies in the relation of maturity and intelligence to the degree of permissiveness in home and school environment, with results that should make even the most conservative educator wonder whether Rousseau's theory is not, at least in part, scientifically confirmed and no mere romantic fiction after all. (See David M. Massie, "Self-Regulation Studies Largely Confirm Summerhill Experiment," *Summerhill Bulletin*, Vol. I, No. 1 [1961], pp. 4–5.)

[5] Recent work on "programmed learning" would be directly opposed to Rousseau's view; so would our ideas of growth as socialization, which derive largely from Dewey; and more generally Rousseau is on the side of readiness rather than challenge when it comes to subject matter.

were, from his very first, successful opera, *Devin du Village*, in an aesthetic, not a dialectical, form.[6] *Émile* is a concrete novel. It is both a romance of education and an expression of an educational philosophy.[7]

II

CHILD INTO MAN

The purpose of the following paragraphs is to reappraise *Émile* as a work of literature, a novel. We expect to show that this is what in fact it is, whatever may have been its author's intention, and to do so by indicating a unity and sequence of plot which are missed if the book is taken as a mere technical treatise.

The central action of the novel is not simply, as the introduction leads us to expect, the success of an experiment in a method of education. The theme is nothing less than human immortality, and the revision of the past. The discovery that this is so emerges as the story develops. The following is offered as a synopsis of the plot.

A certain man, discovering late in life that his own life has been corrupted by the vanity and ignorance of society, so that it has been inauthentic and has contributed little to human progress, determines to rectify this past by creating another

[6] *Devin du Village* was performed for the court by the Paris Opera several times, and in England later. This little opera is an interesting introduction to the later expression and thought of Rousseau: the deliberately simple score has a libretto centering around nature and society. The Village Wise Man, taken into the confidence of a young girl whose fiancé has deserted her in favor of a more wealthy, better-dressed competitor, gives advice by which the fiancé, Colin, is recaptured.

[7] An appreciation of the context in which *Émile* was written, and of its author's intense personal engagement, is found in C. W. Hendel, *Jean-Jacques Rousseau: Moralist* (Oxford, Oxford University Press, 1934, and New York, Bobbs-Merrill, 1963). M. DeMonvel, in his introduction to the Everyman *Émile*, treats the book as a treatise on principles and feels that Rousseau's correspondent who wrote, "I have read your romance on education . . ." wholly missed the point. On the other hand, Professor Hendel's response to our tentative suggestion that the correspondent, not DeMonvel, had located the book in the right genre was "Yes, of course."

self, free of his own vices, who will be the sort of example and parent the author wishes he himself had been. He will thus carry into the future the author's ideal self rather than his actual unsatisfactory self. The central theme, more specifically, is the story of Jean Jacques, who, dissatisfied with the way he himself was trained and his own natural development misdirected, sets about creating in his adopted son and pupil, Émile, the ideal person that Jean Jacques himself might have been, had every social and educational influence in his past been the opposite of what it was.[8] In this combination of the motifs of a Pygmalion myth and the "past recaptured," the father can in a sense relive his own life, give concrete realization to the better possible person he might have been, and bequeath to the future a son who transmits the father's ideal rather than his sad example.

As the story develops, there are repeated episodes of crisis and resolution, which provide direction and interest. We will see, as we offer a summary in more detail, that these crises are of three kinds. There are constant temptations for the tutor to forget his long-range ideal in the interest of his pupil's immediate "progress" judged by conventional social standards, or in the interest of the tutor's own vanity, his desire to impress Émile with knowledge for which the young man is not "ready." There is always — just offstage, in the wings, as it were — the acquisitive, artificial society that surrounds them, threatening to intrude and misdirect; and it is worth noting here that Jean Jacques' elaborate artificial schemes appear when he is, in memory or in fact with his student, on the outskirts of these artificialities of society. As a third factor which offers problems and crises in the plot, there is a duel with nature herself, for there are critical points at which abrupt changes in Émile's interests and rate of growth threaten the enterprise, and the tutor must be a sufficiently skillful "botanist of the

[8] The literary critic may be forced to draw a distinction here between the character of Jean Jacques as it is actually delineated in the book and the biography of Jean Jacques Rousseau himself. For the latter, see the *Confessions* (e.g., Everyman's Library, New York, Dutton, 1931) and the recent study by Frances Winwar, *Jean Jacques Rousseau* (New York, Random House, 1961). On the whole, the author and his character are identical, though the tutor in *Émile* is either more reticent about his past or somewhat more conventional in it than the real author.

self" to recognize these and modify his attitudes and the environment to meet them.

The first book is a soliloquy on the general theme of nature and education, with general notions about human infancy. An infant must be conditioned toward temperance and courage — temperance, by not being allowed to think his will can prevail by the use of rage and tears; courage, by making him familiar with masks and the dark, so that he is spared the fears that night and unfamiliar apparitions would otherwise create.[9] Like delicate plants, infants need tenderness and security; if mothers recognize them as beings of intrinsic value and charm, rather than as nuisances to be turned over to nurses, this will go a long way toward an improvement in society.[10] These reflections establish the theme of the story.

In Book ii, Jean Jacques is living with Émile, who has passed beyond infancy into boyhood. To give nature a chance, the tutor must recognize that there is an intrinsic worth to boyhood; that a natural life for a boy is one in which his desires do not too far outrun his powers, and his lessons come from things, not from commands of persons; and that proper growth requires vigorous outdoor activity. The boy is to learn to use his senses and to discover the laws of cause and effect that limit his power in dealing with things. And the tutor's first problem is to keep quiet, to avoid, for example, scolding or arbitrary punishment if the boy should break a fragile object mistakenly left within his reach. This possiblity is removed in Jean Jacques' case by his living in a rustic cottage with deliberately plain furniture and no ornament.[11] We want Émile, however, to learn some natural sense of "property." For this purpose, he is given a garden, and the result of his invested work is to be his own. This metaphor of the garden runs through the book; the tutor is himself a gardener in a sense, and young Émile will be in contact with growing things as part of his interest in active gardening. "Property," "work," and "title" are elementary social ideas, which Émile is capable of recognizing concretely, but not abstractly. Jean Jacques has arranged an adventure with the gardener, annoyed by Émile's ruining his crop, but willing to give the young man a

[9] *Émile*, p. 30.   [10] *Ibid.*, pp. 13 ff.   [11] *Ibid.*, p. 57.

piece of ground of his own, so long as each respects the fruit of the other's labor.[12]   Here is a first example of the tutor against society, giving his pupil a dangerous concept — before the introduction of civilized notions that cannot be explained as natural. Émile learns from necessity; when he breaks a window, he sleeps in a cold room, until constructive plans can be made to repair it. Jean Jacques neither scolds him nor sympathizes with him but is willing to help with the repair.[13] By example, the ethical lesson is taught that he must hurt no one. Beyond this, contrary to the advice of noted educators of the time, there are no moral lectures or moral judgments.[14] The most important thing that Jean Jacques must remember, which requires considerable reflection to restrain his vanity and conventional notions of "education," is that Émile is *not* to learn symbols alone, to which he cannot attach immediate firsthand meaning.[15]   He will read when he is ready; Jean Jacques offers no books and even passes up the chance to play games with alphabet blocks that lead to quick reading, learned in play.[16] Émile is developing his senses. His judgment and imagination are also growing: there is a beginning of learning experimental physics, at first hand.[17]   Jean Jacques recalls how he had taught a spoiled son of a noble family to exercise by rigged foot races for a cake as prize, after all sorts of verbal admonition had failed to stir the pygmy glutton.[18]   As the sense of sight develops, drawing begins, and the empty walls of the cottage receive some ornament.[19]   Music, taste, and informal geometry continue, and Émile ends his boyhood ready to move on to the acquisition of judgment and common sense.[20]

This is a critical point, for in youth, for a brief span, and for the only period of life, strength grows faster than needs increase.[21]   Boyhood is the age at which Émile thinks in terms of necessity; he sees the world as a set of effects and causes, related in the objective way they are. Youth is the age of interest in utility; Émile begins to wonder what good things are, in addition to his earlier curiosity which concentrated on how

[12] *Ibid.*, p. 62.   [13] *Ibid.*, p. 64.   [14] *Ibid.*, p. 69.
[15] *Ibid.*, esp. p. 74.   [16] *Ibid.*, pp. 80–82.   [17] *Ibid.*, pp. 96 ff.
[18] *Ibid.*, p. 106.   [19] *Ibid.*, p. 110.   [20] *Ibid.*, p. 125.
[21] *Ibid.*, p. 128.

they operated. Adolescence introduces still another dimension of curiosity; it is natural to this age, as it was not to boyhood or youth, to be concerned with what is noble and right, as well as with what is advantageous and what is the case.

As he passes from boyhood to youth, with its sudden spurt in growth and power and its shift in intellectual interest, the increased activity and tempo of Émile's development make it particularly necessary for his tutor to avoid either vanity or error.[22] In the realm of ideas, the student is now able to jump from applied geometry to astronomy, and physics arouses his curiosity.[23] At the same time, since by the end of youth we want him to have learned those virtues that concern himself, and to have acquired some knowledge of nature, this new curiosity affords an occasion for a simultaneous lesson in magnetism and modesty. Jean Jacques arranges with a local conjurer to make Émile interested in magnetism, the secret of a trick with magnetic ducks, and to teach him modesty, as the youth's eagerness to show off his knowledge at the performer's expense ends in discomfiture.[24] It is a successful but difficult artifice. The interest carries forward, and the tutor and student proceed to study magnetism and the vacuum with instruments which they construct for themselves.[25]

Jean Jacques is constantly tempted to offer moral maxims or judgments as to good and bad but holds himself in check.[26] Émile, at this age, is concerned with what is useful, and he begins to question the usefulness of astronomy.[27] Jean Jacques, tempted as any of us would be to lecture on the sublimity and elegance of nature, or to rule arbitrarily that, since astronomy is good, the boy shall study it, has luckily profited from earlier experience as well as from his theory. Like all young teachers, he had once devised a wonderful lesson, one which demonstrated the usefulness of chemistry by detecting the adulteration of wine with litharge. But his student, to whom the concepts of "adulteration," "harmful in the long run," "unfair trade practice," and the like, meant nothing, had been merely bored, despite the tutor's enthusiasm.[28] Jean Jacques, remem-

[22] *Ibid.*, p. 129.   [23] *Ibid.*, p. 134.   [24] *Ibid.*, p. 135.
[25] *Ibid.*, p. 140.   [26] *Ibid.*, p. 141.   [27] *Ibid.*, p. 144.
[28] *Ibid.*, p. 147.

bering his earlier failure, wisely chooses as his demonstration
of the uses of astronomy the rather homey enterprise of having
them find their way back to Montmorency after he has deliberately lost them on an extended hike.[29]

For reading, *Robinson Crusoe* is their favorite (and, indeed,
only) work.[30] And student and tutor commence work on crafts
together; as it happens, Émile prefers carpentry. The study
of crafts includes visits to workshops, and these once more
bring a contact with society and its artificial values. The low
esteem of crafts and craftsmen is a decadent judgment that
Émile must not be allowed to share. At this point it is time
for him to have another lesson in the folly of class distinctions
in aristocratic society, and another example of the preferability
of his own natural way of life. The lesson is an elegant formal
dinner.[31] When Émile thinks the service and conspicuous
waste are signs of greatness, Jean Jacques takes him on a long
walk, ending at a country tavern. As they eat, they recall the
dinner without envy, for their own plain fare is more useful
and tastes better to them.[32] There is a danger from the tutor
again; he is tempted to preach moral lessons, both by criticizing
society's class distinctions and by defending the dignity of
trades; but he does neither.[33]

Émile is by now fifteen. He is not well read, not well
equipped with symbols or half-understood ideas. He has only
those virtues that concern himself, and a thorough knowledge
of nature. His analysis of the illusion of a stick appearing bent
in water is superior to that of sophisticated philosophers, who
have never had his firsthand experience or shared his natural
clarity. The bent stick is another illusion, as the masks that at
first terrified infants were, or the the magic ducks of the
conjuror; adolescence holds still another set of illusions that
will need unmasking.[34]

Adolescence is the stage of life that marks the birth of a
man — a being with passion, and an instinct for reproduction.[35]

[29] *Ibid.*, p. 144.
[30] *Ibid.*, p. 148. It is hard to know how many other books Jean Jacques
would allow today. Surely *The Swiss Family Robinson* and *Boy Scouts
in the Wilderness* would be among them.
[31] *Ibid.*, p. 153.   [32] *Ibid.*, p. 154.   [33] *Ibid.*, p. 155.
[34] *Ibid.*, p. 191.   [35] *Ibid.*, p. 186.

Jean Jacques is convinced that nature still demands modesty and prolonged innocence and that the cultivation of youthful illusions through poetry is not desirable.[36] (Here the reader can add something to the tutor's general reflections by remembering or reading Rousseau's own concrete experience with artistic passion and premature loss of innocence.) It is time for some society. But Émile must see the truth, that the man of the world wears a mask. And just as an infant must not be terrified of masks, so an adolescent must not be envious of them.[37] Here Jean Jacques explicitly compares his raising of Émile to an art of good farming, which does not force the crop: the garden was, as we suspected, a symbol of care for growing things. This has been a central theme throughout the general reflections on nature and education.[38]

At eighteen, Émile is at an age when he must begin to know and live in society. He will be given history, but factual, not romantic. Jean Jacques thinks the model historian for this purpose is Thucydides — Caesar and Xenophon would be at least as good if their whole preoccupation were not campaigns and fighting.[39] Émile is never to wish to be anyone but himself; in reading history, he may admire great men, kings, and generals, but he must not envy them.[40] At the same time, as he becomes aware of society and other men as beings like himself, there is a danger of undue pride, which is quite different from the quiet self-satisfaction we were trying to preserve. When vanity appears, the tutor must repeat the adventure of the conjuror in diverse ways, himself sharing, without comment, in the contrived misadventures.[41] Literature, which is to teach the student of the passions and other persons in the world, may extend to include fables, provided these have no tiresome explicit moral tacked on and do not presuppose the wrong sort of sophisticated manners that have been avoided: the tutor must make an effort to put aside his own taste, and read LaFontaine through his student's eyes.[42] There is to be no rhetoric, by which others are persuaded or deceived into doing one's own will; rather, the natural rhetoric for Émile is to teach

---

[36] *Ibid.*, p. 190.   [37] *Ibid.*, p. 191.   [38] *Ibid.*, p. 193; cf. pp. 6, 216.
[39] *Ibid.*, pp. 199 ff.   [40] *Ibid.*, p. 205.   [41] *Ibid.*, p. 207.
[42] *Ibid.*, p. 210.

him to extend his self-love to others.[43] It is time now for religion and philosophy to be considered by the tutor. This will be the final stage of the intellectual side of the curriculum. Once more, Jean Jacques, however impressed he may be with the philosophy of John Locke and the appeal of the Christian religion, must make an effort to see what is meaningful and suitable for his charge, and he begins by repeating a botanical reflection (one of the few general observations in Rousseau's *Letters on Botany*) that society has replaced the natural pear tree by the dwarf pear in the garden.[44]

Émile is about to know himself and all of nature, and, if he is not dwarfed or enslaved by the knowledge, he will become a man, and friend of his tutor, no longer ward or pupil. Contrary to Locke's convictions, it is wrong to begin with spirits and go on to bodies. From his boyhood on, Émile has known a world of corporeal things, but he is only now beginning to have some notion of an incorporeal "self."[45] Religion would therefore not be sensible for him "at seven or fifteen, and perhaps not at eighteen."[46]

Jean Jacques falls back on his own memories, and the impression made on him by the creed of a Savoyard Vicar.[47] The Vicar, whose beliefs are recounted in twenty pages of compact philosophic writing, has obviously read the work of Descartes. Descartes' *Discourse* is an account, in autobiographical form, of its author's quest for intellectual certainty; he at last discovers that he cannot doubt the proposition "I think, therefore I am," since the doubting would itself be an act of thought. Rosseau's Vicar, however, seems less concerned with intellectual certainty (which depends on our being unable to assert the contrary of a proposition without presupposing it) than with existential certainty. For example, the Vicar is certain (as was Descartes) that he has a self, but he departs from Cartesian types of certainty in his conviction that this self lives in a world displaying power, law, and order; one can doubt this intellectually, but not emotionally. This anticipates

---

[43] *Ibid.*, p. 215.
[44] *Ibid.*, p. 216. Cf. *Letters on Botany* (trans. Thomas Martyn, London, 1785), pp. 33, 48, 72 ff.
[45] *Émile*, p. 218.   [46] *Ibid.*, 221.   [47] *Ibid.*, p. 228.

a distinction we will find of central importance in Immanuel Kant's philosophy and educational theory — between what we can know, as scientifically determined fact, and what we can consistently will, on the basis of moral certainty.

On the same ground of undeniable inner feeling, the Vicar asserts his awareness that his self is incorporeal and has freedom, and that evil comes from this freedom's misuse.[48] He finds grounds for a hope for immortality in the discrepancy between the evidence of an intelligence and a will in the ordering of nature and the frequent failures of justice in individual human lives. Our moral sensitivity would be wholly out of place in a natural order where no future life equalized merits and rewards justly — as our earthly lives evidently do not. (If one takes, against Rousseau, the point of view of some contemporary philosophers, however, the existence of the injustice proves that there is no benevolent will ordering nature, rather than standing as evidence for immortality. This is a point, again, which we will meet in Kant's treatment of religion and religious education.) At any rate, the Vicar cannot reconcile his moral sense and hope for immortality with any barbaric doctrine which consigns all souls born at the wrong place or date to eternal damnation. Indeed, it seems to him incredible (that is, contrary to his most natural moral feeling) that there should be eternal damnation for any soul whatever.[49] Both religious belief and ethics rest finally on man's conscience, an innate love for what is noble, which overcomes his passionate self-interest.[50] For, though self-interest is natural, there is a true self in man which is not identical with his body and his physical existence. "To exist is to feel," but a sensitive soul has a feeling for the good as well as for the comfortable.[51] (On this point, at least, Rousseau is consciously agreeing with the ethical doctrines of Plato and Aristotle.) Beyond this the Vicar cannot honestly go: claims to custody of revelation rest, after all, upon human authority; claims to consensus of mankind for any given religion seem obvious only in the local community where that religion has become established, and the truths claimed as revelation by man's diverse religions are inconsistent with one

[48] *Ibid.*, pp. 244 ff.
[49] *Ibid.*, p. 248.   [50] *Ibid.*, p. 255.   [51] *Ibid.*, p. 253.

another.[52] The Vicar, who had been too long in error (the key to his change of thought seems the discovery that "to exist is to feel," which dissolved his intellectual tendency toward materialism), now is ending his life in "lofty contemplation."[53]

At this point, after their discussion of religion, there is another crisis point, in which Émile becomes a student of Jean Jacques no longer, but a man and friend, in a way that he could not have been had he embraced an obscure philosophy or unnatural, authoritarian theology.[54] Since Émile is a man, the tutor's work, we might think, is now complete. But the story is not over. It will not be over, in fact, until Émile himself has a son, who will learn easily in his family what Émile has learned through the difficult reflection and art of his tutor, and who will carry forward in the human race the "natural man" that Rousseau, too late, wishes he himself had been.

To this end, the old friend still desires not to force nature. There should be a delay of marriage or of vice on Émile's part, and, away from society, the two engage in vigorous hunting.[55] As they share the pleasures of the chase, Émile develops a full awareness of his gratitude for his tutor, and as a friend desires his help.[56] Jean Jacques introduces to Émile the idea of his future wife: it is a romantic, idealized image, which may serve as a touchstone to keep Émile from hasty infatuation and alliance, and it is a needed one, for at last Émile is to be introduced into society — to form his taste, to look for a suitable wife, and to put to final test the power of nature, now almost fully realized, to withstand the social order.[57] Émile does not dislike company but he does not shine as an entertainer or natural leader. "Émile will be, if you like, an agreeable stranger," writes Rousseau.[58] At any rate, after he has formed his taste (Rousseau is still close enough to his younger years as artist to take it as axiomatic that this could be done only in Paris), Émile sets out to the country once more with his tutor,

[52] *Ibid.*, p. 260.
[53] *Ibid.*, p. 257. The passage carries forward Jean Jacques' own memories; cf. p. 232.
[54] *Ibid.*, p. 281.   [55] *Ibid.*, p. 284.   [56] *Ibid.*, p. 290.
[57] *Ibid.*, pp. 293 ff.
[58] *Ibid.*, p. 304, translating Rousseau's *etranger* here as "stranger," which is better than "foreigner."

in search still of his ideal wife, whom they have christened "Sophie."[59] Jean Jacques, as we would expect, has a young lady in the provinces in mind as a perfect bride for Émile, but with complete awareness that he may have misjudged either of the young people and that love cannot be programmed in advance, as lessons in mechanics can. It is, therefore, a fortunate and unpredictable success that Émile and Sophie do fall in love and eventually marry.

The modern reader is not likely to feel strongly persuaded by Rousseau's description of Sophie's education. Rousseau seems to have no acquaintance with girls, in spite of his understanding of women. He manages, unintentionally, to create two Sophies in his novel: one a creature of artifice, the other a girl of natural sweetness. We may see the aesthetic propriety of a polarity of character; as Emile is the man of nature, we might want to present his bride as the extreme of artifice. Perhaps, since all women are weaker than men and more timid, they must live by controlling their husbands cleverly. Thus, we find small Sophie encouraged to choose becoming styles as she dresses her dolls, in order that her own good taste in clothes will be developed when she grows older.[60] Women are to take religion on authority, as their conduct in other matters is to be controlled by public opinion.[61] On the whole, Sophie's girlhood training could be a model curriculum for an M.A. in vanity, flirtation, mendacity, social precocity, and infatuation with heroes of novels. The other Sophie appears when Émile and Jean Jacques actually meet her. Seen through their eyes, she is entirely different from the self-conscious, vain, superstitious little girl that we have just read of. Able to control men by proper femininity, she still retains a natural sincerity that makes Émile fall passionately in love with her (and Jean Jacques, too, as the girl whom he could have loved when he was young). The flaw in the story is, therefore, not fatal or final.

After the marriage, Jean Jacques remains with the young couple as a valued older friend, and the novel ends when Émile

[59] *Ibid.*, p. 320.
[60] *Ibid.*, pp. 321 ff.; 329–330.   [61] *Ibid.*, p. 340.

is about to become a father. The tutor's dream is complete; he has guided nature in the creation of the ideal self he wishes he had been, and he can see his own effect on man's future about to be extended through a child of his ideal and precept, rather than by the mere historical carry-forward of his example.

III

Summary and Criticism

Émile has constantly attracted and educated readers, in spite of their incorrect expectation that it will be philosophic argument, because they nevertheless *feel* the intensity, development, and unity of its "romance" form.

We will return now, for a third time, to Rousseau's ideas on the subject of education. We met them first in the thought of his character, Jean Jacques, who shares them with the reader. Again, we met them in the plot, in which the story of Émile illustrated their realization, in spite of the difficulties that led to the Greek proverb "Fine things are hard." We can now, without being misled by context into taking fancies for facts, stories for syllogisms, recapitulate and appraise them more adequately.

Several crucial ideas that figure throughout are those of growth, nature, symbol, society, spontaneity, and authenticity. In regard to the first of these, growth, Rousseau does indeed seem to have added something true and necessary to the traditional view stemming from Aristotle. There is no reason why a child should be tortured by us and deprived of all present value and meaning in his life because we already view him as an undersized adult and steal his present happiness on the supposed ground that this will lead to enhanced gratification in the future. In fact, in Aristotle's own analysis of nature and growth the growing thing constantly takes on increments of value, so that one could view it as enjoyed attainment at every stage almost as well as one can see it as the frustrated failure to reach full actuality.[62] This idea will recur, in contemporary terms, when we discuss Whitehead's educational philosophy. Rousseau is quite right: no parent or teacher who knows and loves children can feel that a life of disciplined, frustrated practice of adult behavior is good for them — though "civilized" communities may acquiesce in such educational practice because they believe it is a "social necessity."

This brings us to the second of Rousseau's ideas, that civilized society, by an arbitrary caste system, manages to make some men's wills dependent on others', and thus creates an unnatural inequality, a second nature which distorts the true potentialities of man. Much of this seems pure nonsense; it is not true either that children are naturally incapable of recognizing each other as human beings until they are eleven years old or that primitive societies without our elaborate civilization are utopian centers of liberty, fraternity, and equality. In fact, the more primitive they are, the more superstitious and caste ridden they seem, and the farther from Rousseau's saccharine rustic types in his opera. Whether we go as far as Dewey does in seeing self-realization as an essentially social process, or stop at the more moderate view of the Greeks, that effective community membership is a necessary condition for self-realization, we find that Rousseau's case seems one-sided and overstated.

And yet, human nature viewed as latent human capacity can, indeed, be altered — in many ways, including Rousseau's detested forced feeding of moral lectures and words without understanding — into an "unnatural" thing. Émile learns this in his garden in dealing with the care of plants, and Jean Jacques knows how the process works for persons from his own memories. Plastic though it is, human nature, if it develops in its own way, becomes lovable and noble, according to

[62] We note here, in passing, that one theory of "programmed learning" avoids the deadly monotony of "steady input of equal increments of information" by deliberately inserting material out of direct sequence, from time to time, much as a good teacher will digress to show where a lesson is going, or how its problems are treated on a technical level the students cannot yet "fully understand." We might try Jean Jacques' "autobiographical method" to test the need for this digression by recalling what made our own learning experiences challenging and interesting.

Rousseau; and he believes that he can prove it, if his romance of education can make parents and teachers look once more at children in their own right, not as recalcitrant raw material to be forged and beaten into the lead toys of the adult games of "society." That this belief is at least partly justified is evident from the fact that Rousseau's ideas have helped produce lasting educational changes, and some of them are now part of the common sense of our own century.

Rousseau's distrust of meaningless symbols pervades his book. He seems to have an extreme distrust of free imagination, intellectual adventure, or vicarious experience. The reason must be that he has grounded his philosophic certainties in man's natural capacities for feeling, not for thought, and he distrusts symbol and allegory as confusions of the former with the latter. Part of the blame rests with John Locke's enormously popular psychology, which Rousseau accepted insofar as it accounted for ideation. Locke, perhaps justifiably annoyed by the "innate idea" theories of some of his immediate predecessors, argued that the mind is a totally blank tablet; all of our ideas are memories either of impressions made on our senses or of inner states of feeling. To be "meaningful," then, a symbol must refer directly to a firsthand emotion or a firsthand sense datum or set of data. The mind, in Locke's scheme, takes a surprisingly active part in fabricating and creating new complexes of ideas. Given his medical background and empirical bias, we would have expected it to be treated much more mechanically. But for all of that, it is the simple criterion of one-to-one correspondence with sensed or felt components that gives a symbol its meaningfulness for the learner. Error comes in, among other places, in mistaking one set of ideas for another, so that we believe in the existence of winged horses, or think we are Julius Caesar. Rousseau takes this half-truth over and tries to limit what is meaningful by an inventory — a glorified Thorndike word-list — of the "ideas" young Émile has met in his firsthand experience. To evaluate this, we need some notion of how often, and how seriously, a child mistakes a symbol or fiction for a reality, and how detrimental such mistakes are. Even without any judgment on this point, however, it is very doubtful that ideas are ever "met." The model of the mind as a box filled with snapshots of individual sensible substances is of extremely limited use. The "meaning" of an idea surely lies partly in its value as a tool whose use gets results, as Dewey will show. Viewed in another light, it is significant for the meanings of other ideas that are related to it, as Aristotle argues. Finally, it may remind us of a universal — an ideal or type, as Plato observes. The shielding of Émile from the romance of encounters with ideas beyond his immediate and full comprehension is not remedied by a half-hearted and unconvincing provision for the development of artistic creativity. (For instance, he draws some pictures of trees as a boy, and goes to Paris to finish perfecting his "taste" as a young adult.) It is by no means clear that "natural feelings," so sheltered from contact with other human beings and society, however "pure" they are, will not be wholly undirected, indiscriminate, and empty.

It must be clear from these remarks that Rousseau's notions, except for the first one we discussed, that of growth, are seriously at odds with other educational theory, with what seem subsequent findings of empirical inquiry, and with what we are intuitively likely to accept as making sense in our society. Yet, granting this oddity, and certain real limitations, no one who has read Camus, or Sartre, or Heidegger, or Dewey, or Skinner can deny that Rousseau is talking about ideas that are peculiarly relevant to education today. Sometimes he is not "scientifically exact," most of the time he is not saying things that seem sensible, but when we consider the idea of "authenticity," a modern name for "nature," we can't escape an uneasy feeling that, though he doesn't seem sensible, Rousseau just could be right. Man, in his quest to know himself, must give up the attempt to equate his true identity with the mask he wears, the social role he plays. It is always tempting to give up the search, to check our freedom at the door, and to play the part of a "typical" social role — the teacher, or postman, or violinist who knows what is expected of him and shocks no one by acts of nonconformity. It is even possible, as Socrates saw in Athens and Sartre in Paris, for social beings to come to believe that they *are* the masks they wear, the roles they play. The more society sets up fixed types, classes, categories, and patterns of conformity, the more one needs a dash of the "noble savage" to remain human — to feel authentically, not merely to respond to stereotypes as a rat does to his learned conditioning. All of our American stress on youth, which might at first seem just what Rousseau wanted, tends — from Junior Achievers Clubs to Boy Scouts — to transpose the categories, motives, and pressures of adult society to the child's level and start conditioning early for the adult choice not to be a person, but to be a thing. Intimidation, anesthesia, hypnotism by the superhighway and subway and endless assembly line destroy our capacity for feeling. And if, as Rousseau's Vicar believed, to exist is to feel, civilization in its progress may threaten to destroy human existence altogether. In our summary of *Émile*, the reader who feels that we have falsified Rousseau's own notions by highlighting masks, conjurors, and illusions is invited to look closely at the author's own emphases in his story, and at its recurring themes.

A good deal of abstract verbalization appears in our texts and journals today about something called "Existentialism as a Philosophy of Education." We might think Rousseau, with his romantic "nature," the very antithesis of such a modern position. But, if only we read "authenticity" for "nature," we find *Émile* almost the only properly concrete existential protest against inauthentic roles in the educational literature today.

The student of educational theory should recognize the difference between a story — "Paul's Case," *The Magic Mountain, The Brothers Karamazov*[63] — and a properly philosophical analysis or argument. The argument can be translated, abstracted, and paraphrased; it aims at a meaning which is impersonal, clear, and universal. But the story makes its point in a different way; perhaps here the function of the philosopher or critic is to suggest to the reader the sort of unity, sequence,

[63] Willa Cather, "Paul's Case" (in *Death and the Bright Medusa,* New York, Knopf, 1920); Thomas Mann, *The Magic Mountain* (trans. H. T. Lowe-Porter, New York, Knopf, 1938); Fyodor Dostoyevsky, *The Brothers Karamazov* (trans. Constance Garnet, New York, Modern Library, 1950). All three are "stories of education" and in this sense as much the property of the expert in education as of the literary scholar.

and thought that he himself has found, then retire while the student reads, or chooses not to read, the novel.

Suggestions for Further Reading

There are several translations of *Émile* available in English. The one cited in our essay is by Barbara Foxley, Everyman's Library, (New York, Dutton, 1911). Another, somewhat abridged but with a good concluding commentary, is William Boyd, *Émile For Today* (London, Heinemann, 1956). The principal works of Rousseau which bear on *Émile* are *The New Heloise* (London, H. Baldwin, 1784), *The Social Contract* (ed. Charles Frankel, New York, Hafner, 1951), and the *Confessions* (available in several translations; e.g., London, 1796, reprinted in Everyman's Library, New York, Dutton, 1931). This last, Rousseau's account of his own life, gives a vivid picture of a career whose perils he would like to train Émile to avoid.

C. W. Hendel, *Jean-Jacques Rousseau: Moralist* (Oxford, Oxford University Press, 1934, reprinted in paperback, New York, Bobbs-Merrill, 1963), is an excellent introduction to Rousseau's philosophical development and thought. Frances Winwar's biography, *Jean Jacques Rousseau* (New York, Random House, 1961), is a good popular presentation. Two other biographies, each of which has a chapter devoted to *Émile*, expose its sources in Rousseau's own life: *Jean-Jacques Rousseau*, by Matthew Josephson (New York, Harcourt, Brace, 1931), and *Jean-Jacques Rousseau*, by Jules LeMaitre (trans. Jeanne Mairet, New York, McClure, 1907).

The reader who wishes to pursue commentary on *Émile* further should read William Boyd, *The Educational Theory of Jean Jacques Rousseau* (London, 1911). A more fine-grained study is that of Peter Jimack (in Theodore Bestermann, *Studies in Voltaire and the 18th Century*, Vol. XIII, Geneva, Institut et Musée Voltaire, 1960). For a brief statement of Rousseau's relations to his contemporaries, see Ernst Cassirer, *Rousseau, Kant, Goethe* (Princeton, Princeton University Press, 1945). Irving Babbitt's classic statement of the humanist position, *Rousseau and Romanticism* (Boston, Houghton Mifflin, 1919), has been reprinted in paperback by Meridian Books (New York, Noonday Press, 1955).

The reader who thinks that Rousseau is too heavy-handed in his critique of society as mindless and personality-destroying may want to read contemporary examinations of the same problem, indicating how acute it is: *The Lonely Crowd,* by David Riesman, Nathan Glazer, and Reuel Denney (New Haven, Yale University Press, 1950, and New York, Anchor Books, 1956); *The Organization Man,* by William H. Whyte (New York, Simon and Schuster, 1956); *The Status Seekers,* by Vance Packard (New York, McKay, 1959); *The Man in the Grey Flannel Suit,* by Sloan Wilson (New York, Simon and Schuster, 1955). Rousseau's protest was largely naturalistic and romantic. Contemporary protests are more urban and dramatic. See Jean-Paul Sartre, *Nausea* (trans. Lloyd Alexander, Norfolk, Conn., New Directions, 1959), and Albert Camus, *The Stranger* (trans. Stuart Gilbert, New York, Knopf, 1946) and *The Plague* (trans. Stuart Gilbert, New York, Random House, 1948).

CHAPTER FIVE

Kant: *The Moral Structure of Education*

I

KANT AS THE BRIDGE BETWEEN THE CLASSICAL AND CONTEMPORARY VIEWS

The eighteenth century was dominated by the concept of order. Newton published the *Principia* in 1687. A hundred years later Kant brought the concept of order to a climax in the field of philosophy. He was the first philosopher since medieval times to ask himself about the significance of the order demanded by scientific thought for human thought in general. He was the first man whose mathematical insight and scientific enthusiasm were closely coupled with philosophical disposition and humane concern. Not till the time of Alfred North Whitehead do we find again this rare unity of talent and concern.[1]

[1] It is, however, due in part to fortunate historical accidents that this concern and talent were turned to the theory of education. A statute of the University of Königsberg required periodic lecture courses on *Pädagogik* to be given by the Professor of Philosophy, and Kant delivered these lectures at least in 1776, 1781 (the year of the appearance of the first edition of his *Critique of Pure Reason*), and 1783 (the year of the *Prolegomena to Any Future Metaphysics*). Kant's notes were edited and published in 1803 by F. T. Rink, who mentions in his introduction that the original assigned reading, a textbook by Consistato-

The major problem of Kant's philosophical maturity is how to deal with this triumph of the idea of natural order. The mechanism implicit in much seventeenth-century thought had smoothly, but swiftly, become a mechanistic determinism, and the world a rationally ordered world whose ultimate contingencies can be traced to the nature of sense experience.[2] There was thus an increasing suspicion that sense did not portray things as they are but only represented them in a roughly consistent way. One form of this view Kant shared, and wisely insisted upon. For if we do know things in themselves, and not just their appearances, and all things in themselves are determined by natural law, there is no freedom; and without freedom a moral choice is impossible. In a thoroughly deterministic world all choices are coerced by the past and are neither blamable nor praiseworthy.

Kant knew that it was a fault of his predecessors to suppose that the observed world could be regarded as a model for all aspects of reality, observed or not. Moral experience has a directly observable side to it. We perceive men's actions and judge their motives accordingly. But we do not observe their motives directly, nor do we even observe our own directly, for observation necessarily includes a sensory content, something seen, or felt, or heard, and so on. Yet moral consciousness and perceptual consciousness lie side by side in the same total consciousness, and moral and perceptual experience are abstractable from one another only by a certain dissective violence.

Thus Kant's scientific determinism was mitigated by his doctrine of the world as acted upon. He held that insofar as an act is a concrete physical fact it can on principle be explained

---

rialrath D. Bock, had been found by Kant entirely inadequate in its theoretic grounding. (See I. Kant, *Über Pädagogik*, ed. Dr. F. T. Rink, Königsberg, 1803, p. iii. This edition is cited hereafter as Rink. Other citations of the *Lectures on Pedagogy* refer to Annette Churton's translation, first published in 1899, reprinted in paperback as *Education*, Ann Arbor, University of Michigan Press, 1960.)

[2] Even the philosophical doubts of that arch-skeptic, David Hume, as to the demonstrability of causal necessity had no effect on his belief in a causally fixed external world; see, for example, his rejection of chance in the *Treatise of Human Nature*.

in terms of scientific determinism. As a thing it is not one whit different from the fall of a tree, the eruption of a geyser, or the greening of a spring pasture. But an act has its origin on the side of motivation, and a motive is not itself an object of scientific investigation, for motives in themselves lack the sensory content that would bring them under scientific scrutiny.

This, then, is the first thing we need to notice about the world of Immanuel Kant. It is a deterministic world to the extent that it is merely an object of knowledge. But to the extent that the world is an arena of action, the agency of moral action may lie in the rational self and may therefore be free, i.e., self-determined (not undetermined). The real contrast is between an acting self which is other-determined and one which is self-determined. Even the free act makes its innumerable concessions to what nature and circumstances require. The crucial question is, "Did the core cause, the central reason for the act, come from within the person, or was it planted there by external events from which he did not disentangle himself?"

The second thing we need to notice about Immanuel Kant is that he is unaffected by a doctrine of biological evolution. There were evolutionary theories aplenty in Kant's time. But they were theories of the evolution of society, or political order, or the earth, and so on. Kant himself was the author of an evolutionary theory of the origin of our solar system which, partly modified, is widely accepted by contemporary astronomers. But there was no clear-cut and widely received doctrine of human evolution. Kant is something of an oddity to us, then, a man surely with a "modern" mind, who is nevertheless not confronted with the necessity for dealing with the demands of evolutionary theory. He is thereby separated from the moderns Dewey and Whitehead. On the other hand, Plato and Aristotle did not have at their disposal the scientific knowledge which resulted from the new view of nature as being a massive and intricate machine whose processes obeyed strict mathematical laws. Newton had shown the great power of this approach to what happens in physical nature. For a hundred years between Newton and Kant the scientific world planted and reaped in the fields that Newton had plowed. The scientific successes of the seventeenth and eighteenth centuries arose from a combination of patient observation, shrewd mathematical application, and brilliant theoretical formulation that laid the groundwork for the deterministic view of nature.

We thus have a man who, like the Greeks, was concerned with the fixities of human nature and regarded the development of humanity as the outcome of the complex interaction of man, nature, and society. On the other hand, Kant, like all the men of the Enlightenment, believed in at least a modified form of the doctrine of progress. It is not too much to say, in an aside, that the doctrine of progress probably did more to prepare the intellectual climate of nineteenth-century Europe for the emergence of a doctrine of biological evolution than any one other single factor.

Now of what educational significance are these facts about Kant? Progress takes two forms: intellectual, i.e., the advancement of learning and understanding; and moral, i.e., the improvement of society and the human spirit. In the minds of the men of the late eighteenth century there had been a major breakthrough in the former area: Observation, analysis, grouping, generalization, all come from the side of experience; from the side of thought come logic, mathematics, and the capacity to bring theory into focus with brute fact. Moreover, there was a further hope, which comes to be explicit in the nineteenth century, that the control over nature would decrease the misery of the mass of humanity and that the groundwork for a happy society would be thus laid.

The crucial problem, then, is how to obtain moral progress. This is the area in which Kant is most interested in his lectures on pedagogy. He rightly concentrated his attention here, for all knowledge is useless and even harmful unless it be backed up by character. Briefly, the answer is this: Moral progress depends on the combination of freedom and discipline in the individual, and on the substitution of the ideas of duty and the public good for those of power and state solidarity in the minds of the public authority. This latter theme is common, though sporadic, in the *Lectures on Pedagogy* but is found throughout Kant's writings, wherever the topic is admissible.[3]

---

[3] See, particularly, the essay "What Is Enlightenment?" (trans. L. W. Beck), in *Foundations of the Metaphysics of Morals and What Is Enlightenment?* (New York, Liberal Arts Press, 1959), pp. 85–92.

The *Lectures on Pedagogy* are more sustainedly concerned with the moral individual than they are with the moral public authority, however. "Our ultimate aim is the formation of character," says Kant.[4]

Kant is thus more than a bridge between classical and contemporary theory. He is also more than a spokesman for an era. He is a serious reminder that *the aim of education is first to develop a human being with a sense of dignity and duty*.

Accordingly, Kant restrains himself from the specificities of curriculum and even subject matter in order to focus on what he knew to be the primary concern, the maturation of a human person. The *Lectures on Pedagogy* are of primary interest in the philosophy of education merely for the subject matter with which they concern themselves, even if we wholly reject the conclusions. Consequently, the numerous trivial weaknesses of the *Lectures on Pedagogy* should not deter a serious student. It is true that far too much ink is spilled on the subject of mother's milk and that the notes are patchy, often exhibiting minor inconsistencies of terminology. Nevertheless, Kant's *Lectures* must be read for their vital emphasis on moral education.

II

The Import of Kant's Major Philosophical Works

Scientific Knowledge

Kant's first great work, *The Critique of Pure Reason*, is an essay in the scope and limits of human knowledge insofar as that knowledge is founded on sense experience.[5] It starts with a problem: Both in mathematics and in science, we seem in fact to have some knowledge which is certain, which applies to experience and yet is independent of it; that is, no experi-

---

[4] *Education*, p. 98 (Rink 116).

[5] Kant, *Critique of Pure Reason*. Citations will be from the abridged Modern Library translation of Norman Kemp Smith (New York, Random House, 1958), with the pagination of Kant's first and second editions (A and B pages) in parentheses.

ence would undermine its certainty. If all we knew were simply records of past experiments, however, these records could never give us necessity and absolute certainty, only high probability.[6] An example of what Kant has in mind is the proposition that two plus two equals four. Now, we do not in fact try to test this proposition experimentally, and it seems clear that no possible laboratory experiment would increase or weaken our certainty that four is, and must be, and always will be, the sum of two and two. Yet if this statement were simply a record of past experiment or experience, we could not be certain that it would *always* hold. Further experiment or experience might strengthen or weaken our confidence in it, as happened in the case of the nineteenth-century notions about the "aether."

Of course, some logicians and mathematicians would object to Kant's example on the ground that two and two are four is not a case of "knowledge" in Kant's intended sense. For, they might argue, a statement such as "A is A" tells us nothing new about A; and "two plus two" is simply another name for "four" in a "formal language," namely, that of mathematics. Consequently, while it cannot be false, it cannot be informative, either. Kant meant by knowledge, however, something that added new information to our starting points, not simply saying "A is A" in various guises. Kant would therefore explicitly deny the objection, saying that "two plus two" is *a*

---

[6] In the *Prolegomena to Any Future Metaphysics*, a work designed to clarify the *Critique of Pure Reason* (which had, Kant felt, been completely misunderstood by various readers and reviewers), Kant develops this distinction between analytic and synthetic a priori knowledge in detail, as the central distinction in the *Critique of Pure Reason*. The *Prolegomena* is cited by page in the edition of Paul Carus (La Salle, Ill., Open Court, 1902), which has a number of interesting supplementary sections on Kant; the revision of this translation by L. W. Beck (New York, Liberal Arts Press, 1951) has some advantages as a translation, however, and includes pagination from the Berlin Academy edition of Kant's *Works* (23 vols., 1900–1956). Kant was clearly aware of the difficulty of communication of his philosophy (see *Prolegomena*, pp. 149–163); he regards even the *Prolegomena* as suited primarily for future teachers of philosophy. It seems highly probable, therefore, that in the 1783 version of his lectures on education he would have tried to avoid philosophic technicalities and novelties, though he would certainly have had his own system in mind in founding the basis of his own educational philosophy.

direction for constructing something, not just the name of a number; and we find that two plus two is four only when the construction has been completed. That this is so is clear cut in complicated mathematical operations which have predictive certainty. In other words, mathematics is informative as well as necessary.[7]

Without following this issue further, however, we may note that there are other examples of Kant's claim. There are kinds of knowledge which are not generalizations from experience. Indeed, once they are understood, we may say that experience must conform to them, not vice versa. For instance, there is the rule that *every event has a cause.* A scientist never asks, "Was there any cause of this event?" He asks, rather, *what the cause was.* And if we should raise the other question, whether there was any cause at all, it becomes clear on reflection that no experiments could answer it, since the experiment is intended to *reveal* the causes.[8]

Kant offers us a new explanation of these cases of certainty: These statements cannot be about things in themselves (for things in themselves by definition would have to be things as unrelated to anything else — but things known are, to the extent that they are known, related to the knower). Such statements really reflect the nature of the human observer. Space, time, substance, causality — these are the common ways through which observed things make themselves known to us, that is, not as they are in themselves, but as they are related to us, as known to knower.[9] They are spatially spread out, endure through some portion of time, have a substantial unity, and are causally interdependent. By definition, therefore, scientific knowledge is not concerned with "noumena," i.e., things in themselves, but is instead a knowledge of things as

[7] For the modern status of the controversy over the analytic or synthetic character of mathematical knowledge, see Stephan Körner, *The Philosophy of Mathematics* (New York, Hillary House, 1960), esp. pp. 25–32 ("Kant") and 119–156 ("Mathematics as the Activity of Intuitive Construction").

[8] The status of "causality" as a Kantian category will be treated below; see n. 11.

[9] Kant described this reorientation as a new "Copernican revolution." *Critique of Pure Reason*, pp. 15–17 (B xvi–xviii).

they appear through the complex lenses of human observation.[10]

Kant's proof of this claim is intricate and difficult.[11] But any intelligent observer can watch these basic modes of human understanding develop in the growing child. As we learn more about child psychology, we see that awareness of space, time, things, and causes, and finally of self-identity, emerge progressively and must emerge with the intellectual growth of the child.

Let us begin with the "blooming, buzzing confusion" of the infant's world, as William James so well described it. At this stage the infant exhibits diverse but chaotic sensitivity. For example, there is no association as yet of a bright red color and a soft or hard tactile feeling; the infant will not reach for things it sees. "Space" as a way of organizing sense-experience is still in abeyance. Bit by bit, we find the baby recognizing "things," reaching for and tasting the bright objects he sees, beginning to recognize a parent or a rattle as the same thing it was on last appearance. But there is still little of the idea that things stay the same or that events have causes, if we can trust what we see. For when the rattle is taken away at first, apparently for the baby it has simply stopped existing; he is sad

[10] "Things in themselves," as the entities we think of as causes of phenomena, recur frequently in Kant; see especially *Critique of Pure Reason*, p. 149 (A 235–236).

[11] Kant's proof (the "transcendental deduction" of the categories), by which he claims to establish that coherent, self-conscious experience over any period of time depends on our use of twelve patterns that order the "representations" which we perceive successively, is very technical. Different versions are offered in the first and second editions of the *Critique*, and there has been controversy over their relative merit. The point is discussed and both versions are given in the Norman Kemp Smith edition, cited above, pp. 81–106. The table of Kant's twelve categories appears on p. 72. Our present purpose is *not* a transcendental deduction to show that these and just these categories are necessary. We are rather offering some considerations from what Kant would call "empirical psychology," plus some applications to the study of child development, to show that in human development they are successively acquired. The reason for this modification of Kant's argument is not merely that the present formulation is simpler, and more pertinent to education, but also that there is some doubt as to whether Kant's argument does exactly prove the necessity of just these categories, as he thought. See below, n. 13.

at its loss but cannot wonder where it is now or why it went away. He has not yet learned to organize his sense-images in patterns of thing ("substance") or cause. It is some time before the young child is aware of the fact that he is an individual, with a self which is other than "objective things." The distinction between a thing and its appearance to me, between myself and an outer world, requires the use of a complex pattern within which I sort out (1) my own subjective impressions, (2) the objects of which they are impressions, (3) the causal connection between those objects and my representations of them, and (4) the relations of those objects and impressions to my own past experience.[12] The two final necessary mental patterns that emerge in the youth as he matures are (1) curiosity as to what lies beyond the boundaries of experience, an interest in ultimate first causes ("How did the world begin?"), smallest elements ("What is the world made of?"), and so on, and (2) a sense of responsibility that comes from recognizing himself as causing good or bad things to happen when he wills them to. The world as a whole and himself as a moral agent become the basic factors in his thinking, however implicitly.[13]

Kant's point is this: Unless our fundamental and automatic methods of ordering and interpreting sensation were effectively the same, we could not have continuous and coherent experience of an adult sort at all, nor could adults live in a common world. The "methods of ordering and interpreting" emerge in the development of the human capacity to understand. Since these methods are the primary way in which we order our coherent experience, (1) they are necessary for *any* experience, which is why we feel or recognize the irrelevance of testing their validity *by* "experimenting," and (2) what the "thing in itself" as apart from the "thing as we experience it" is like, is necessarily a question science cannot answer.

---

[12] The distinction of objects from appearances, an essential component in my recognizing my self encountering something other which is given, is treated in some detail in *Critique of Pure Reason*, pp. 96 ff. (B 140 ff.).

[13] The "Ideas of Reason" which tempt us to try to pass the limits of possible experience, are the central concern of the *Critique of Pure Reason*, pp. 161–306 (A 295 ff.).

When we come to the final two great phases in the development of human understanding: (1) philosophical curiosity and (2) awareness of our freedom, the situation is changed. All of the content of scientific and factual experience comes by way of sensation. But in asking about God, freedom, immortality, and so on, my ideas stretch beyond the limits of all possible experience, and I cannot find a final answer. Worse than this, my "reason" (which prompts me to ask these questions) has the ideal before it of a closed complete system, which would answer such problems, but my "understanding" (the faculty that orders sensations into experience) can only proceed step by step, by a method of fitting pieces together. Any answer I can "understand" will seem to me *unreasonable*, yet any reasonable answer must seem *incomprehensible*.

For example, it seems unreasonable to me that the world has no first cause, for an infinite regress of things changing, each changed only because it is acted on by something earlier, could never even get started: like a row of dominoes, each of which knocks over the next, the series must start somewhere.

On the other hand, if I take the alternate supposition that there is a beginning point, a first cause, I run into an opposite difficulty: What caused the first cause to act? The idea of something which is *a* cause but is itself *un*caused clearly violates the rule that started my thinking about causes in the first place, namely, that every event is caused. Either way I turn I can only seem to get an unreasonable answer!

Kant called problems of this sort "antinomies."[14] In general, his solution was that we get into these problems by asking questions about a totality which we could never possibly experience. Thus in the example given, the task of finding causes in nature is set before us as a mode of procedure, but one without an end. That this *task* is unending, however, does not warrant our asking questions about unending or terminating series of causes *themselves*, for we have no knowledge of things in themselves.

---

[14] See *ibid.*, pp. 253–264; *Prolegomena*, p. 92. In an Appendix to the *Prolegomena* (pp. 157–158) Kant challenges his critics to find any flaw in his proofs of these contradictions between understanding and reason, as a test for his system.

Although I have no knowledge of things in themselves, I do have an awareness of a thing in itself, namely, my self as that which is confronted by a moral choice. My consciousness is not confined to my knowledge of the external world. This is the world of objects known. I am also subjectively aware of myself as a being which must choose how to act, and this being is never an object of scientific knowledge, for it is never sensorily given. Clearly, we all have moral concerns and uncertainties, and a sense of responsibility, however minimal. The "inner" self quite escapes scientific accountability, yet is there as the entity which asks, "What ought I to do?"[15]

Scientific explanation, to make sense, must be prepared to explain each event as the outcome of causes before it; and not only can I not observe any "freedom" in my laboratory but I discover many causal factors that influence any human decision, e.g., heredity, environment, social conditioning, and so forth. We might therefore suppose that in principle human behavior is completely subject to causal determinism. The reason lies in the limits of scientific observation: "Human behavior" as the scientist observes it must be seen as space-time sequences capable of causal order; his *objective* point of view screens out or hides some relevant dimensions of human nature. My sense of duty, on the other hand, is a moral certainty, not a scientific fact; but it is a set of ideas and concerns that could not be explained even if the natural world of the scientist offered all that it might offer as to what a man is.

Moral Knowledge

We have already seen that science deals with phenomena: things as they appear in forms we can understand. And science is our only responsible method for discovering matters of knowable fact. Yet we can think that our certainty of freedom reflects some truth about man as a thing in himself; we may actually *have* responsibility without being able to observe it scientifically.[16] Kant is here asserting that different

[15] For the antinomy of the free or un-necessitated cause, see *Critique of Pure Reason*, pp. 253 ff.

[16] Kant at this point offers an interesting remark: One might think that this "introspection" would permit a responsible observation of one-

ways of knowing are involved in science and in ethics, and that no good can come from confusing a known scientific fact with a known moral certainty. I do have freedom; but I can't understand how I have it. My being confronted with my freedom is of an entirely different sort from being confronted by the physical world about me.

The reader who has followed our introductory summary of Kant's philosophy this far will recognize what he meant when he wrote, in the *Critique of Pure Reason,* "I have therefore found it necessary to deny knowledge in order to make room for faith."[17] Certainly, Kant did not suppose that he must deny all knowledge. What he *did* deny was the extendibility of scientific understanding into the realm of morality. Moreover, although morality can be self-justifying without appeal to religious dogma *or* scientific dogma, the presuppositions of morality, namely, the conceptions of freedom, immortality, and finally God, carry moral inquiry into the area of religion. Morality has a rule which is reasonable without appeal to religion, but the concepts it employs, if we persistently analyze them, carry us into the field of religion. Moreover, religion that pays no attention to moral matters is worthless. Kant writes in a biting passage,

> Religion without moral conscientiousness is a service of superstition. People will serve God by praising Him and reverencing His power and wisdom, without thinking how to fulfill the divine law; nay, even without knowing and searching out His power, wisdom, and so on. These hymn-singings are an opiate for the conscience of such people, and a pillow upon which it may quietly slumber.[18]

One wonders how directly these words of a religious man led to those of a fanatic atheist, Karl Marx, who held that religion

---

self, at least, as a "thing in itself." But introspection is of two kinds: If I look at or into myself "objectively," I am in a sense standing outside, peering in through the lenses of natural science; if I am aware of a sense of dignity when I am, as a single self, exerting my will in a good action, I may well be in this case realizing some aspect of my true and undivided self, but only subjectively, in "unscientific" introspection. See *Critique of Pure Reason,* pp. 178–210.

[17] *Ibid.,* p. 22 (B xxx).   [18] *Education,* p. 113 (Rink 134).

was "an opiate of the people." Thus religion stands on one side of morality as the home of its ideals, and science stands on the other, as describing the world within which morality must act. What, then, is the meaning of moral freedom?

Man as a being that acts can have a sense of responsibility only if he has some sense of an ideal. He has some freedom to make a difference in the world by what he wills only if he is led to set aside his pleasure and security when he acts as he ought. He must also be free to choose the opposite course, however, setting ideals aside, and, following instinct and inclination, capitulate to the natural order as though he were not free.[19] An animal, on the other hand, seems to behave wholly predictably in following his "interests," that is, his drives for survival (both personal and species) and satisfaction. It is hard to think of a flat worm, or for that matter a chimpanzee, as becoming neurotic from tension between his interests and his responsibilities. Man, however, is somewhere in between an animal and his own ideal of a self-determined being generating his destiny rather than yielding to it.[20] As an animal he has instincts, drives, a desire for happiness; as reasonable, he can see that his choices make a difference, and that if he chooses to give up his freedom, he is relinquishing part of his true moral identity. A free will is creative. By its own decision, it does not simply passively follow an external causal law but creates a new law relating what *ought* to be to what *is* through its action. While I may accept suggestions, I am free only if I legislate for myself; and if I am compelled to do what (someone else sees that) I ought by punishments or bribes, I have been coerced, since I have not acted on my own responsibility and through my own freedom.[21]

[19] The following discussion is based largely on Kant's *Foundations of the Metaphysics of Morals*, trans. L. W. Beck (see n. 3), supplemented by the *Critique of Practical Reason and Other Writings in Moral Philosophy* (trans. L. W. Beck, Chicago, University of Chicago Press, 1950, and New York, Liberal Arts Press, 1956). The former, published in 1785, may be closer to Kant's ethical ideas in 1783 than the latter, a more elaborate treatment, published in 1789.

[20] We deliberately put this Kantian point in non-Kantian language, since it serves to show the way in which the child may be exhibiting early groping toward a moral ideal of a self-determining man when he discusses what he will be when he grows up: "engineer," "pilot," and so on.

[21] *Education*, pp. 87–88, for example.

My possession of reason and freedom, in other words, sets me apart from the rest of nature and gives me a peculiar dignity and task so long as I do not give these up by default — i.e., by choosing to act as if I were not free.

The "moral law" which constitutes my ethical ideal is unconditional, and Kant presents it in three forms, calling it the "categorical imperative."[22]

The three rules Kant offers to judge the rightness of an action are these:

1. Always so act that the basic principle of your action could be a universal law (the same for any man confronted with your choice).

2. Always regard human beings as ends, never as means only.

3. Always act so that your action could be a precedent for the law of an ideal society.

These conditions guarantee that there will be no confusion between our *selfish interests*, in which we are at the mercy of some particular set of events, and what can be reasonable claims and actions that hold under all circumstances and all events. If we are guided by a self-determined principle which is invariant from one circumstance to another, and from one rational person to another, we may well be forced by different circumstances to *apply* the rule differently (I may give one man the benefit of a free charity, the other not, for example), but they must not force us to change the principle itself. If the basic principle which I apply is determined outside me, then I am not free.

Our sense of morality thus presupposes a concern to find general rules to which neither we nor others are exceptions, to recognize that what is right is so, regardless of person, place, or time; that human freedom must therefore be respected in others as well as in ourselves; and that consequently it would be irrational not to direct our actions toward the common welfare. But notice that our moral sensitivity is possible *only* because of our freedom to create a moral order. Freedom cannot belong to us as parts of nature, and it lies beyond any limit of "human nature" that science can discover. We exercise this higher power whenever we will to be reasonable and do what we ought, independent of our instinctive inclinations.

[22] *Foundations of the Metaphysics of Morals*, pp. 55–57.

It is important to notice that reason *always* makes a demand for universals. In scientific study it demands universal laws which all *physical* things obey. In moral practice, it demands a universal law which all *moral* things obey. The idea of obedience to a law is thus deliberately ambivalent, belonging to both morals and science. Both fields use the words "obey" and "law." The difference lies in this: The physical object obeys because it is coerced, must do so. The moral subject obeys — insofar as it is moral — because it espouses and embraces the law of reason. For to espouse the law means that, although it *can* abandon the commitment to laws as such and subside into being just another *object*, it chooses to obey them. To be human is to realize one's freedom *and* one's respect for duty. It is the task of moral education to bring about such realization by providing experience in making responsible decisions.[23]

Now, the second formulation of Kant's ethical rule, that we show respect for human dignity in *every* being like ourselves, leads him to distinguish two types of operation of the will. On the one hand, when, using my freedom, I choose to act in a way that creates what ought to be in the realm of nature, obeying an ideal that I legislate for myself, my will has "autonomy," that is, authentic self-determination. However, if I make my decision because of fear of punishment or hope of reward, this is not a free, self-responsible moral choice; rather, it is "heteronomy," determination of a will, not by itself, but from other, outside pressures. We yield to such pressures at the price of giving up our freedom and our dignity, and it is intrinsically *immoral* and *disrespectful* of the principle of man's moral freedom for us to try to make one man's will wholly subject to another's.[24]

The being who chooses to give up his freedom becomes a part of "nature," a "phenomenon," and, as phenomenon, may deserve and require coercion and punishment to restore him to awareness of his true responsibility and status.[25] A being that

[23] *Ibid.*, p. 29.

[24] *Ibid.*, p. 53; see also "What Is Enlightenment?"

[25] In Kant's later work, *Metaphysische Anfangsgrunde der Rechtslehre*, (a translation of which is forthcoming from the Liberal Arts Press under the title *Metaphysical Elements of Justice*), there is an unexpected realism: Kant treats the responsible human agent who has chosen to relinquish dignity for interest and to forego respect for other men, in terms of pressure, deterrence, and control almost reminiscent of Hobbes.

cannot achieve, or has not yet achieved, awareness of freedom
and duty is "phenomenal," hence requires kindness, restraint,
and disciplined direction, but cannot claim our respect for its
right to autonomy that an adult human being can. The early
stage of child training is one in which the child's capacity for
freedom is recognized but is not given premature license.[26]

Knowledge of Purpose and Design

In his third and last Critique, the *Critique of Judgment*, Kant
asks why man is such a strange amalgam or combination of
piecemeal understanding and creative reason.[27]   Science cannot answer. Indeed, in terms of pleasure or survival, reason,
with its unanswerable questions and its reminders that a good
action must be one that anyone else could also do, seems a
liability. An innate sense of *purpose*, which we cannot justify
ethically or scientifically, makes us *hope* that there is some
order in cosmic history which can reconcile the anomaly of
man's being grounded in, yet reaching beyond, the phenomenal
order of nature. Kant himself is inclined to think that some
salvation through the gradual perfection of an immortal soul
would be the most credible religious hope. Once in a while, in
contemplating works of fine art or in seeming to see evidence
of purpose in nature, we have the feeling of seeing something
as a whole, not merely picking up its properties piece by piece
through scientific understanding. But in the last analysis, the
conciliation of science and ethics in a religious vision remains
neither a scientific fact nor a moral certainty, but a pious
hope.[28]

Just as the first Critique gives us a frame of reference for

[26] *Education*, pp. 18–21, 23–24, 31–32, and elsewhere.
[27] This is the central theme of the *Critique of Judgment* (trans. J. H.
Bernard, London, Macmillan, 1892; reprinted New York, Hafner Library
of Classics, No. 14).
[28] Beauty and purpose, and our human sensitivity to them, are topics
of the two major sections of the *Critique of Judgment*. It is interesting
to see what Kant thought was *plausible* (though certainly not demonstra-
ble) as a picture of the solar system in his early *Allgemeine Naturge-
schichte und Theorie des Himmels* (*Universal Natural History and
Theory of the Heavens*), Book III. Books I and II present the essentials
of the Kant-Laplace hypothesis; Book III treats of the probable characteristics of the inhabitants of other planets than our own.

*intellectual education, and the second Critique supplies us with
the larger context for moral education, the third Critique, in
its way, provides the basic notions for a rationale of religious
hope.*

III

Applications to the Art of Teaching

The central theme — or tension — which this necessarily extended introduction to Kant's lectures underscores is that between what we might call the "natural" and the "ethical" man.
We learn to use our reason through restraint and discipline,
initially through discipline, progressing as rapidly as exercise
and experience can bring the forms of adult thought into
active operation.

Two immediate qualifications are necessary, however. (1)
Ideally, "If we wish to establish morality, we must abolish
punishment."[29] But if punishment is required, it should be
based on the child's desire to be loved and respected. Mere
physical punishments or those "inflicted with signs of anger"
are without worth.[30] (2) "We must, however, form in children
the character of a child, and not the character of a citizen."[31]
The same is true of the child's knowledge of the world, and of
the development of his understanding.[32] This lesson of graded
development, of patterns appropriate to the child's age, Kant
learned from Rousseau. A revival of this often-neglected ideal
appears in both Dewey and Whitehead, but in the light of the
theory of evolution.

The most *efficient* routes to intellectual development, by
way of "discipline," presume a learner who is being externally
conditioned and taught by itemized, programmed learning.
Since the learner is not being consulted in his choice as to
whether he will or will not recognize a true responsibility to
learn, he develops his "cleverness" at the expense of sensitivity
and freedom.[33]

[29] *Education*, p. 84.   [30] *Ibid.*, pp. 88–90.
[31] *Ibid.*, p. 85.   [32] *Ibid.*, pp. 31–32, 93–94.
[33] "Cleverness" not only is different from intelligence but may be
detrimental to its possessor; see, for example, *Foundations of the Metaphysics of Morals*, p. 21.

One of the very first sentences of Kant's lectures anticipates the problem: "The human child requires discipline" because "it desires to be free."[34] The contrast between discipline and freedom presents an apparent practical dilemma. Moral development requires experience in situations that provide for and respect freedom of choice — no will ought to be ("heteronymously") subject to another — and this, as Bertrand Russell appreciatively noted, includes the wills of children. But if the student does not choose the course of discipline which science and the teacher find most efficient in the development of his skill and understanding, and is then immediately punished and coerced back into conformity, what conclusion will he be entitled to draw as to our own real respect for freedom, and when and by what means will he develop independence and moral character? The ideal may well be the student who accepts conditioning because of high morale: he wills for himself to do what his teachers suggest will add to his intellectual maturity. But the actual student (plus or minus one standard deviation) seems rather to act from heteronymous motives. Approval (not respect, which is often greater for the "individualistic" student), college admission, future status, money from the family for high grades — these persuade the youngster to easy adaptation and pursuit of pleasure, and he drifts along, choosing only to drift, with no training in the exercise of, and hence no realization of, his inalienable freedom at all.

Returning to the *Lectures on Pedagogy*, one becomes aware at once of the philosophical problem of the education of a human self. The problem can be stated as follows, with a minimal use of special Kantian terms.

1. Insofar as we are concerned with man as part of nature, that is, as a phenomenal being, scientifically exhaustible, the most efficient way to educate him is reinforced conditioning; in this role he is a complicated white rat.

2. Insofar as we are concerned with man as a moral agent, a dimension which eludes science and is unique in nature, the one thing we must avoid is reinforced conditioning, since the self-realization we seek is not conformity to external pressure, nor is it comfortable facility with concepts, but awareness of responsibility for one's own free choice.

[34] *Education*, p. 4 (Rink 4).

3. The high school student (to take the swiftest period of transition as an example), as noumenon, is entitled to our respect of his dignity and freedom; as phenomenon, not yet completely "human," he still requires our constant coercion and bribery to insure his efficient mastery of the forms of cognition.

4. The greater our stress on discipline of the subject matter, the less likely we are to reach adequate respect for freedom; the greater our stress on freedom, the less likely we are to find our students using that freedom with intelligent and experienced anticipation and planning of the consequences of their motives.

5. THEREFORE, what fraction of the high school student is, and what fraction should be, noumenal and what fraction phenomenal is perhaps the most pressing problem confronting the theory of secondary education.[35]

In the *Lectures* themselves, Kant is concerned with the progressive self-knowledge and self-realization of a human being born with a desire for freedom, but without the knowledge or sensitivity needed to *be* free. Four things stand out in the educational needs of infants and children. They arise as projections of Kant's general philosophical position.

1. Experience must be regulated, even at the earliest age, so that habits are formed which will not run counter to the later need to make ethical decisions. In this Kant harks back to the classical teaching of Aristotle. We must not allow an infant or child to learn that it is able to control other wills by its own interests. This habit would lead to a wrong view of autonomy, and of the causal relation of will to reasonableness and objectivity. But there is no gain in "breaking the will" of a child; any reasonable and possible request should be agreed to.[36]

2. The most effective punishments will be of two types. The first is the establishment of a negative causal connection between the end that the child has in view and the unreasonable

[35] In this connection, it is interesting to compare the amusing novel by Vercors, *You Shall Know Them* (Boston, Little, Brown, 1953, currently reprinted as *The Murder of the Missing Link* New York, Permabooks, 1961), which is about an English court trying to determine whether "tropis," a tribe of Australian manlike animals, are or are not "human."

[36] *Education,* pp. 53–57.

means used in his (or her, understood throughout) attempt to attain it. The small child who hits a playmate to get a toy should not be permitted to keep it. The second type of punishment is withdrawal of approval. Since already the latent exercise of freedom gives the child a certain self-respect, he will not choose to repeat actions that forfeit this respect from others, particularly others toward whom he has affection.[37]

3. The sense of morality requires that the child's world be one from which he learns the lesson of human equality in respect to dignity. He must not be allowed to treat servants, for example, as instruments of his will, or to feel that they or any social groups or classes are less human (that is, less entitled to freedom or less deserving of respect) than his parents and himself.[38]

4. The child should grow up with some experience of duty and responsibility as part of the family; some regular duties, expected of him, are a part of his ethical education.

Turning now to intellectual development, it is clear that this is equally essential if there is to be adequate self-knowledge, effective citizenship, and correct recognition of the consequences of actions. The points where Kant's philosophy shows through distinctively in his treatment of this aspect of education are as follows:

1. We have already noted Kant's insistence, particularly in his first *Critique*, that human knowledge requires the interplay of concepts and intuitions, neither of which is intelligible without the other. The constant demand that learning include application of what is learned (conceptually) to firsthand experience and concrete instance is a direct corollary of this fundamental idea in the critical philosophy.[39]

2. Kant's discrimination of three intellectual "faculties" (or

[37] *Ibid.*, pp. 90–91, 104; and compare Kant's essay, "On a Supposed Right to Lie from Altruistic Motives" (included in L. W. Beck, ed., *Critique of Practical Reason*, the University of Chicago Press edition only); but see also Beck's Introduction to the edition of *Foundations of the Metaphysics of Morals*, cited above.

[38] *Education*, p. 119.

[39] *Ibid.*, pp. 74–75. Kant is here applying to *"Pädagogik"* the central thesis of his critical philosophy, which he summed up in the statement, "Thoughts without content are empty; intuitions without concepts are blind." (*Critique of Pure Reason*, A 51, B 75.)

"functions" of the mind, if we prefer modern terminology), judgment, understanding, and reason, is fundamental to his educational psychology.[40]

In an example of logical thought, such as the inference:

> All extended bodies have weight.
> Air is an extended body.
>
> Therefore, air has weight.

we see these three operations of the mind at work. The general concepts of weight, body, and extension are formed by the understanding, classifying, and relating of sense experience in general patterns and according to rules. That the proposition "Air is an extended body" falls under the general case of "All bodies are . . ." is an act of *judgment.* If, instead of "air," the subject of this second proposition were "this red pencil," the feeling of judgment as recognizing sense-data as instances of concepts would be clearer. That the conclusion follows from the premises which tell us why it holds is an operation of *reason,* which always "seeks something unconditioned" — a necessary and complete chain of thought "explanatory" of its theorems. "There must be reasons" is a sound Kantian slogan; and these reasons lead on to other reasons.

The child must, therefore, learn to generalize, through relating concepts to their relevant instances, and to see systematic relevance between the universal and the particular.

Here, unfortunately, Kant's more technical philosophic views lead him to *oversimplify* the needed formal side of this emergence of understanding. For he seems to us now to have been far too dogmatic in his convictions that Euclid had completed geometry for all time, as Newton had physics and Aristotle had, much earlier, logic — and as Kant himself had completed the theory of knowledge. The resulting *certainty* on Kant's part that precisely twelve basic categories of thought[41] must always order human experience, and that in-

[40] *Education,* pp. 79 ff., where Kant lists the "higher faculties" in the technical terms that marked the major divisions of the *Critique of Pure Reason:* ". . . *die Kultur des Verstandes, der Urtheilskraft, und der Vernunft"* (Rink, 88).

[41] Substance, cause, reciprocity; possibility, actuality, necessity; reality, negation, limitation; unity, plurality, totality.

telligence is just the ability to use these, oversimplifies the formal aspect of education, science, and philosophy dogmatically and drastically. It is here that the nonevolutionary character of Kant's thought is most evident. As he envisaged no evolution of human nature, but rather its fixity, he also envisaged no evolutionary possibility for the *basic* structure of human knowledge.[42] For instance, on scientific grounds alone, even the modern materialist would prefer to regard the category of substance ("thing") as derivative and the category of "event" as basic, since matter is analyzable into patterns of vibratory occurences, and the fundamental particles are nothing but chains of such occurrences.[43]

3. The intellectual growth we have been discussing requires a proper substructure of physical development, for both intellectual and moral purposes, since it requires discipline in its most easily recognized form. Kant is clear (as Plato was before him and Whitehead after) that active play at intervals furthers effective learning.

4. Point 2 on page 117 is pedagogically very tempting, for if Kant's view were right, programmed learning could be set up scientifically, so that the student would quickly be led to conceptual mastery of the formal laws governing nature, space, and time, and we should be a long way toward accepting the idea of teaching machines.

5. We have seen why, in Kant's view, science cannot answer ethical or religious questions, the *reasons* relevant to which we cannot *understand*. If we believed that our methods of understanding nature applied to ethics and religion as well, the idea

[42] Ever since Hegel, one philosophical generation after Kant, philosophers have argued on various grounds that while something in the nature of categories is indeed necessary, different cultures and different stages of science may use others than Kant's own dozen. For example, while "causality" as a pattern exactly fits the needs of Newtonian physics in Kant's own time, contemporary science may find "correlation" or "determinate probability" a more fundamental and useful notion. For some later developments of Kant along this line, the writings of C. I. Lewis, Henry Margenau, and Ernst Cassirer are particularly suggestive. The category of "substance" has had its fundamental character challenged both by linguists and by A. N. Whitehead; see n. 43 below.

[43] For the impact of this substitution of "event" for "substance," in a modern account of human nature, see our Chapter Seven, "Whitehead: The Rhythm of Nature."

of "responsibility" would appear unscientific and false, and our religious visions untestable if not fictitious altogether. The student must not be encouraged to adopt an attitude of scientism or hyper-intellectualism; his skill, and his trust in knowledge, must yet, as Kant indicates in the preface to the second edition of his first *Critique,* leave room for faith.

As for moral education, we make progress in ethics, if we do at all, on the basis of other aspects of the educational situation than those of the class recitation or the laboratory. We must cooperate and act with other human beings and so recognize both our own practical freedom and the likeness of others to ourselves — which gives them equal claim to moral value. Television education or teachers' methods which make the presence of other human beings dispensable in favor of machines have special handicaps to overcome, since the social character of learning is thereby minimized and may be erased. The risk is especially great with the young child.

Finally, beyond ethics, in that dimension of education which treats of religion, a child should be told about adult hopes and beliefs in terms to which he can respond from his own sensitivity to and experience of affection, coherence, and purpose. Holding, as Kant does, that doctrines cannot pose as laws of empirical science, and that religion is in fact destructive of morality if it presses us into doing as we are told by threats of pain or promises of pleasure, he suggests that some concepts of "natural theology" are all that the child's judgment can respond to without error or confusion. Thus the image of God as a father whom we love is an example of what makes judgmental sense to the child; the story of this God sending a she-bear to devour the children who teased a prophet because he was baldheaded does not.[44]

In conclusion, three things stand out in Kant's *Lectures on Pedagogy.* The first is the reflection, in simplified form and almost inadvertent, of the most abstruse ideas of the Kantian philosophy in an order which parallels their emergence in the three great *Critiques.* The evidence for this is double: first, the apparently casual introduction of terms which have a tight meaning in the more rigorous philosophic frame; second, an

[44] *Education,* pp. 113–115.

order of development of topics that reproduces Kant's own successive lines of inquiry, as we move from fact to freedom to faith both in pedagogy and in his critical philosophy.[45]

Second, the design of learning to bring about maximum intellectual effectiveness seems to Kant a far more simple and scientifically controllable enterprise than almost any other educator has ever thought it to be. As long as we attend to the necessary complementarity of form and content, as well as concept and intuitions, the formal structures of mathematics, science, logic, and philosophy seem to Kant to have been isolated completely and clearly, so that they could be quickly and scientifically taught by proper programmed discipline.[46]

Third, when we confront a free moral agent, we cannot simply impose our alien will, no matter how useful this may be to society. We expect such an agent to act in a way guided by self-respect and his duty toward others.[47] There must be espoused commitments, not imposed ones, even if the imposed ends be the right ones. This tension might reasonably be called the "pedagogical antinomy." It rests on a philosophic problem that lies beyond the reach of scientific testability. The actual human infant, let us assume, is wholly phenomenal; the ideal adult has fully attained a noumenal self, beyond phenomena; but what is a high school student? How far should he be indulged in his desire to make his own decisions, as long as he

[45] It seems that Kant, at least in his 1783 set of notes, embodying his intention to go beyond Bock's textbook, already had in mind the strategy of the three *Critiques*, though the second was not completed until 1788, the third not until 1790. Since *Foundations of the Metaphysics of Morals* in 1785 shows that the ethical dimension had already occupied Kant and been clearly outlined, this is primarily interesting for its relation to the third *Critique*. It is also, of course, crucial for the interpretation of the *Lectures on Pedagogy*.

[46] See *Education*, p. 72; but also pp. 13–14, and above, n. 42. This is another case in which the reader wishes he had been given *reasons* as well as *recommendations,* for Kant recommends the "mechanical method" (with maps and pictures) for geography, rejects it for languages (in the interest of his principle that forms without content are empty), and expects it to become possible for history as better programming is developed. But in spite of this variation in practical judgement, it is absolutely clear that if "thought" depends only on twelve categorical patterns, the recognition and use of these could be taught "mechanically" with startling efficiency, once they had been identified and isolated.

[47] *Education*, pp. 100–103.

respects the same right in others?[48]   And, for that matter, how literally did Kant mean his opening remark (however much he later qualified it) that even a human child "desires freedom"?

Suggestions for Further Reading

Kant's philosophy, like Aristotle's, is difficult to master; it is a model of patient analysis, but full of technical terms and distinctions. The exceptions to this generalization are his writings on ethics, politics, and education. For Kant's philosophy in general, S. Körner's *Kant* (Baltimore, Penguin Books, 1955) is excellent. A briefer presentation is given in N. P. Stallknecht and R. S. Brumbaugh, *The Spirit of Western Philosophy* (New York, McKay, 1950), pp. 342–380, 454–461.

Kant's ethical essay, *Fundamental Principles of the Metaphysic of Ethics* (or *Morals*), is not tech cal and is interesting reading, in spite of its formidable title. It is translated as *Foundations of the Metaphysics of Morals* with the essay "What Is Enlightenment?" by L. W. Beck, with a good introduction (New York, Liberal Arts Press, 1959). Two other works that are interesting and not overtechnical are *Perpetual Peace*, in various translations (e.g., that of L. W. Beck, New York, Liberal Arts Press, 1957), and *Religion within the Limits of Reason Alone*, with an essay by John Silber (New York, Harper Torchbooks, 1960).

Of Kant's more technical works, the *Critique of Pure Reason* in Norman Kemp Smith's translation is recommended; the Modern Library (New York, Random House, 1958) has this for the major part of the work, with translations of both the first and second editions where they differ, and an excellent introduction. Kant presents his own more popular version of the argument of this Critique, proving that reason is forced, on self-examination, to recognize its own limitations, in his *Prolegomena to Any Future Metaphysics*. We are by now familiar enough with Kant's type of argument to follow this simplified version rather easily, though he himself, when he wrote it, thought its degree of difficulty made it suitable "for future teachers of philosophy." The Open Court edition of the *Prolegomena* in Paul Carus' translation (LaSalle, Ill., 1902) has interesting supplementary material; L. W. Beck's recent translation (New York, Liberal Arts Press, 1951) is also excellent. The *Critique of Practical Reason* (trans. L. W. Beck, New York,

[48] *Education*, pp. 20–21 (Rink 24–25).

Liberal Arts Press, 1956) and *Critique of Judgment* (trans. J. C. Meredith, New York, Oxford University Press, 1952) are also available.

The translation of the *Pädagogik* lectures (reprinted as *Education*, Ann Arbor, University of Michigan Press, 1960) is now somewhat out of date, and the reader able to do so will profit from reading the German, either in one of the editions of Kant's collected works or in Rink's 1803 edition.

From Kant's investigation of the way in which the mind imposes form on the content given through sensation, new philosophical theories of symbolic form have taken rise. The classical study in this tradition is E. Cassirer's three-volume *Philosophy of Symbolic Forms* (New Haven, Yale University Press, 1957); a briefer, less technical, and very interesting presentation is Suzanne Langer's *Philosophy in a New Key* (Cambridge, Harvard University Press, 1942).

CHAPTER SIX

Dewey: *The Educational Experience*

There is a present tendency in so-called advanced schools of educational thought . . . to say, in effect, let us surround pupils with certain materials, tools, appliances, etc., and then let pupils respond to these things according to their own desires. Above all let us not suggest . . . to them what they shall do, for that is an unwarranted trespass upon their sacred intellectual individuality since the essence of such individuality is to set up ends and aims.

Now such a method is really stupid. For it attempts the impossible, which is always stupid; and it misconceives the conditions of independent thinking.[1]

Man can progress as beasts cannot, precisely because he has so many "instincts" that they cut across one another, so that most serviceable actions must be *learned*. In learning habits it is possible for man to learn the habit of learning. Then betterment becomes a conscious principle of life.[2]

I

PROGRESSIVISM AND THE IDEA OF PROGRESS

Dewey is the one philosopher in whom philosophy and educational theory are virtually indistinguishable. No philos-

[1] "Individuality and Experience," *Journal of the Barnes Foundation,* Vol. II, No. 1 (January, 1926), p. 4.

[2] *Human Nature and Conduct* (New York, Holt, 1922), p. 105 n. Reprinted by permission of Holt, Rinehart and Winston, Inc.

opher has written so extensively on education. In civilized countries between the two wars he left his mark everywhere, not only in the Western Hemisphere, but in Turkey, China, and Japan as well. Even in Russia Dewey was well received until the time of his vindication of Trotsky against Stalin.[3] Plato alone competes with Dewey for having shaped contemporary civilization educationally; and Plato's influence comes by way of a series of modifications beginning with Aristotle.

The very richness of Dewey's educational writings may lead to some confusion. For all his systematic exposition of ideas, he is not the author of a system. Only broad outlines can be made out, and even then the variety of Dewey's thought is such that opposed ideas can be hauled out of context and made to give a scrambled picture.

Dewey's writings lend themselves to ambiguity. There is another problem in Dewey's educational philosophy: his writings coincide with the rise of so-called "progressive education." Thus, in the popular mind, and often in the professional mind, the name of John Dewey and that of "progressive education" have been far too firmly linked. These problems and misunderstandings require that we not only place his educational thought in the context of his philosophical views but also rescue him from his critics and disciples.

Our approach to Dewey is indicated by the two quotations given at the head of this chapter. They show that a common confusion about Dewey must be avoided. Dewey can be — must be — called a *progressive*. He firmly believed in progress, both actual and possible. Like William James, he believed that ours is a world of real gains, real losses, and hence real risks, within which, through the exercise of his intelligence, man can better himself. This faith in the human capacity for human self-perfectibility is the best that secular education has to offer. In Dewey's case it survived two wars and a great economic depression,[4] and its mood dominates the only work he ever

[3] George Z. F. Bereday, W. W. Brickman, and Gerald H. Read, *The Changing Soviet School* (Boston, Houghton Mifflin, 1960), pp. 67–69.

[4] *Reconstruction in Philosophy*, enlarged edition (Boston, Beacon, 1948), introduction.

devoted to the subject of religion.[5] Growth, development, evolution, progress, betterment — these are ever in Dewey's mind and often at the end of his pen. In this sense he was progressive.

Dewey's interest in progressive *education* is at most that of an ally in respect of common objectives. Insofar as progressive education is impatient with the static conception of what is worth learning, insofar as it is concerned with the continuity of the growth process, insofar at it stresses the early interrelation of manual discipline and intellectual discipline, and insofar as it knows that education accepted without interest is not education at all, Dewey is its friend. But where what calls itself "progressive education" becomes a hands-off-let-the-bud-unfold technique, or slips into a dogma of its own, or tends to confuse amusement with education, Dewey no longer subscribes to it.[6]

The confusion of Dewey as progressive with Dewey as concerned with progressive education has obscured Dewey's true place in contemporary education. Worse, it has lent the authority of America's greatest educator to some of her most flagrant educational excesses, since there is no copyright on the title "progressive educator." As we unravel this confusion, we will find a way into the heart of Dewey's philosophy, along a route peculiarly significant to his educational philosophy. At the core of Dewey's philosophy lies what he calls "the experiential continuum." We shall deal with this notion largely as it bears on the educational process, proceed from it to the idea of habit and the self, the relationship between knowledge and consciousness, and return to education as a social process.

We move from an educational problem in method to the philosophy of education; we then return to the status of education in society. This approach is particularly apt in the case of John Dewey. There is no pendulum in his lifework between education and philosophy, but only a mutual reinforcing

[5] *A Common Faith* (New Haven, Yale University Press, 1934), esp. pp. 71 ff.
[6] For a review of these subjects, see *Experience and Education* (New York, Macmillan, 1938), pp. 1–22.

polarity, since "If we are willing to conceive education as the process of forming fundamental dispositions, intellectual and emotional, toward nature and fellow men, philosophy may even be defined *as the general theory of education.*"[7]

II

PROGRESSIVE EDUCATION

Early in this century Dewey recognized the dangers implicit in the "unfolding bud" theory of education.

It will do harm if child-study leave in the popular mind the impression that a child of a given age has a positive equipment of purposes and interests to be cultivated just as they stand.[8]

The child is expected to "develop" this or that fact or truth out of his own mind. He is told to think things out, or work things out for himself, without being supplied any of the environing conditions which are requisite to start and guide thought. . . . It is certainly as futile to expect a child to evolve a universe out of his own mere mind as it is for a philosopher to attempt that task. Development does not mean just getting something out of the mind. It is a development of experience and into experience that is really wanted.[9]

We will return later to the theory of experience. For the moment we will concentrate on the apparent quarrel between the traditional and the progressive approaches to education.

Progressive education is quite capable of placing too much emphasis on freedom: "It is not too much to say that an educational philosophy which professes to be based on the idea of freedom may become as dogmatic as ever was the traditional education which is reacted against."[10] Unlike the social utilitarians, Dewey rejects the idea of freedom as freedom to do as

[7] *Democracy and Education* (New York, Macmillan, 1916), p. 383.
[8] *The Child and the Curriculum* (Chicago, University of Chicago Press, 1903; Phoenix Books, 1956), p. 15.
[9] *Ibid.*, p. 18.
[10] *Experience and Education*, p. 10.

you please, provided you do not get in the way of your neighbor and his freedom. This purely negative meaning of freedom may indeed be constitutionally guaranteed, for citizens in a democracy. But there is a positive side to freedom as well. It must be won. We are certainly not to present the young child with unlimited choice in his self-development. Freedom is not even a coming-of-age present: "Freedom," says Dewey, "*or individuality,* in short, is not an original possession or gift. It is something to be achieved, to be wrought out."[11]

Dewey means by "freedom" the target of education and not its foundation, if freedom be the privilege of being nondirected. Moreover, he holds this view with regard both to discipline by the curriculum and to discipline by the teacher. In a little-known pamphlet published by the League for Industrial Democracy he is explicit about the values of the conservative tradition: "The 'Three R's' are at all times the tools for introduction into higher studies; they have to be mastered if further initiation is to occur."[12] Again and elsewhere, "It is a ground for legitimate criticism, however, when the ongoing movement of progressive education fails to recognize that the problem of selection and organization of subject-matter for study and learning is fundamental."[13] It goes without saying that the student is hardly fitted for making the selection.

As it is with curricular content, so also with teacher supervision and planning — in short, with discipline from above. Only an extreme "either-or philosophy" discards the ruling role of the teacher merely because education has in the past been routinely authoritarian. "On the contrary, basing education upon personal experience [that of the students] may mean more multiplied and more intimate contacts between the mature and the immature than ever existed in the traditional school, and consequently *more, rather than less, guidance by others.*"[14] More guidance, then, and by better-trained teachers. The real plea in Dewey is for the better-trained teacher, and therefore for a "science of education." But even here Dewey

[11] "Individuality and Experience," p. 6; italics ours.
[12] *Education and the Social Order* (New York, League for Industrial Democracy, 1934), p. 3.
[13] *Experience and Education*, pp. 95–96.
[14] *Ibid.*, p. 8; italics ours.

has been misunderstood, for "science" is not supposed to refer to something modeled on physics or mathematics, but is rather "the existence of systematic methods of inquiry, which, when they are brought to bear on a range of facts, enable us to understand them better and to control them more intelligently, less haphazardly and with less routine."[15]

The need of such a science as the special equipment of the trained teacher — upon whom the progressive movement at its best places a greater burden for understanding and supervision than did the traditional — is a principal reason for the multiplication of schools of education throughout the United States. The most common — and justified — charge against these schools has been that they emphasize method at the expense of content. Long before the pendulum had begun to swing back toward the teaching of substantive content to young teachers who had been drilled in method (but were deficient in the knowledge of the subjects they taught) Dewey issued a clear warning:

> Failure to perceive that *educational science has no content of its own* leads, on the other hand, to a segregation of research which tends to render it futile. The assumption, if only tacit, that educational science has its own peculiar subject-matter results in an isolation which makes the latter a "mystery" in the sense in which the higher crafts were once mysteries.[16]

Dewey draws richly upon the Platonic tradition, especially upon the Seventh Letter and the *Republic*, when he affirms this point in still another way: "The net conclusion of our discussion is that the final reality of educational science is not found in books, nor in experimental laboratories, *nor in the classrooms where it is taught,* but in the minds of those engaged in directing educational activities."[17]

Here are three doctrines, then, often proposed as examples of "progessive education," which Dewey not only does not support but condemns: (1) self-development through student choice of materials (as in the "advanced schools" Dewey

---

[15] *The Sources of a Science of Education* (New York, Liveright, 1929), pp. 8, 9.
[16] *Ibid.*, p. 50; italics ours. [17] *Ibid.*, p. 32; italics ours.

speaks of); (2) nondirective supervision on the part of the teacher; (3) an educational science with a content of its own. "There is no spontaneous germination in the mental life," says Dewey.[18] The seed must come from somewhere — if not from the teacher then from other sources less consciously aware of the influences which they have.

Since the excesses and even some of the less questioned features of modernism in education get so little support from Dewey, we should ask, "What exactly does Dewey reject in the traditional education?" The many answers which we can find in his work reduce at last to two closely related ones: (1) "We educate for a static social order which does not exist."[19] The forces of ferment and change in society do require a relatively stable basis, a sea anchor. But the sea anchor may become a bottom anchor; our stabilities may take on the shape of a dogma which is the denial of the fundamental possiblity of progress.[20] What is required as between the school child and his society is "keeping alive the ordinary bonds of relation."[21] We are thus led back to the subject of the experiential continuum, which refers not merely to the continuous experience of Homo sapiens as a race but also to the continuous interrelations among the various parts of existing society. (2) The other great failure of the traditional scheme is this: "It imposes adult standards, subject-matter, and methods upon those who are only growing slowly toward maturity. The gap is so great that the required subject-matter, the methods of learning and of behaving are foreign to the existing capacities of the young. They are beyond the reach of the experience the young learners already possess."[22] Here is one of the great points of coincidence with Whitehead, namely, that each phase of development in the human organism has its own natural proprieties and needs, its own values and interests whereby it grows into its world; but these phases are integral

[18] "Individuality and Experience," p. 5.

[19] *Education and the Social Order*, p. 9.

[20] See especially *The School and Society* (Chicago, University of Chicago Press, 1900; reprinted with *The Child and the Curriculum*, Phoenix Books, 1956) for an expansion of this theme.

[21] *School and Society*, p. 76.

[22] *Experience and Education*, p. 4.

to total growth and have neither mere instrumental value in preparing the child for the status of adult nor an utter independence from the social order, with which they are actually interdependent.

What, then, is the true meaning of preparation in the educational scheme? In the first place, it means that a person, young or old, gets out of his present experience all that there is in it for him at the time in which he has it. When preparation is made the controlling end, then the potentialities of the present are sacrificed to a supposititious future. When this happens, the actual preparation for the future is missed or distorted. The ideal of using the present simply to get ready for the future contradicts itself. It omits, and even shuts out, the very conditions by which a person can be prepared for his future. We always live at the time we live and not at some other time, and only by extracting at each present time the full meaning of each present experience are we prepared for doing the same thing in the future. This is the only preparation which in the long run amounts to anything.[23]

Traditional education fails because it tears the student out of his changing society and divorces his concerns from the interests proper to the various stages in his growth.

So much for the squabble between the traditional and the progressive approaches to education; they require something other than the discovery of each other's weaknesses to support their own convictions. We shall have to look beyond the squabble itself if we are to bring together the two types of insight and avoid the perils of choosing up sides.

III

THE EXPERIENTIAL CONTINUUM

To write about Dewey's philosophy of experience is to write about his philosophy. We cannot go far with the one without encountering the other. Of progressive education he wrote that it needed, "in an urgent degree," "a philosophy of

[23] *Ibid.*, pp. 50–51.

education based upon a philosophy of experience,"[24] and shortly spoke of the "experiential continuum."

The experiential continuum has two aspects that are significant for education: the continuity between individual and society, and the continuity between mind and matter, between thought and things. Dewey resembles Plato in seeing that neither the individual nor society experiences in utter independence of the other. Again, we have no knowledge of a mind which works independently of matter, i.e., the brain, yet all matter is apprehended through some mental activity. Let us see what each of these aspects of the experiential continuum has to do with education.

1. In broad outline Dewey's social and political thought can be presented as a peculiarly American synthesis of nineteenth-century English and American views. British individualism in political thought is of the skintight sort. Each man's individuality is as distinct from another man's as the body enclosed within his skin. It is at its best in the political tradition of personal right, the theory of ownership, and the conception of *personal* responsibility for *public*-mindedness in *public* affairs. Persons tend to be treated as insular, with bridges of obligation to other islands. A community is only a collection of individuals, and it is nothing other than the achievement of these individuals. A pattern of custom survives the individuals, to be sure, but it is authored and authorized by them. John Stuart Mill's "Essay on Liberty" brings this theme to a climax.

Over against this view is its converse, climactic in Hegel. In Hegel the wholeness of a people is assignable to the unitary spirit which expresses itself through them. World history "represents the rationally necessary course of the World Spirit, the Spirit whose nature is indeed always one and the same, but whose one nature unfolds in the course of the world."[25] The primary entity in Hegel's world is the Idea, manifested as World Spirit and further manifesting itself through the individuals. The World Spirit unfolds through the lives of persons. They die, but it lives in the continuity of race and species.

[24] *Ibid.*, p. 19.
[25] G. W. F. Hegel, *Reason in History* (trans. Robert S. Hartman, New York, Liberal Arts Press, 1953), p. 12.

The World Spirit is in a sense the only true individual. "For us, then, a people is primarily a spiritual individual."[26] Now what of freedom in such a picture, where the World Spirit continuously lives in the transient generations of peoples? ". . . Freedom of Spirit is the very essence of man's nature. [Yet] World history is the progress of the consciousness of freedom."[27]

The British tradition emphasizes freedom as a native right, a property of man simply because he is man. Hegel says yes, it *is* of the essence of man (not of his existence), and the progress of history is toward actualization of this freedom through consciousness. We are instantly struck by the remark of Dewey quoted above: "Freedom or individuality . . . is not an original possession or gift. It is something to be achieved, to be wrought out." It is the task of education to provide the conditions under which an individual emerges toward his privilege of freedom, *not* merely to assume individuality or freedom for what is only a person in the making. Both the British theme and that of Hegel must be taken into consideration.

Is society nothing but a group of individuals? Or are individuals just what society makes them? Americans tend to answer yes to the first question and no to the second. In the nursery school we see a certain stage of social development in which the society is merely a group of individuals. Each child may build his own house of blocks alongside other children. One child does not help another, and the teacher sees to it that no child interferes with another. Is American social life still in the nursery school stage of parallel play? Has it refused to advance to the stage of recognizing and profiting from interdependence? On the other hand, was it an exaggerated Hegelianism in Hitler's Germany that led to the notion that the German people is everything, the individual German is nothing? (*"Du bist nichts, dein Volk ist alles."*)

The problem of individualism versus collectivism is an old one in political debate, and it bears directly upon education. What politicians neglect is its philosophic foundations. Isn't it true that I must in the last analysis depend upon what I hear and what I see in order to understand and act? What some-

[26] *Ibid.*, p. 52.   [27] *Ibid.*, p. 24.

body else says or claims cannot be accepted if it goes against my own perceptions. Yet isn't it equally true that apart from my common life with other men I can gain very little that is knowledge? The so-called idealist, who concentrates his attention on the ideational factors in knowledge, will point out that what we perceive really depends upon the interpretative framework. This interpretative framework, whereby we understand what we perceive, is the inheritance of millennia of intellectual achievement, that the child educationally inherits. Imagine a human child reared by animals, then suddenly placed in a large city. If he survived ten minutes he would go mad before he could find a place to hide. Almost nothing would make sense. And consider how primitive the mere ability to stay out of harm's way is as compared with the abilities and breadth of understanding of an educated man. Yet all these things depend upon the vast corporate resources of society as a whole. Does an individual, apart from others, gain knowledge? Are his private views of much value if they can stand no sort of public test? Finally, are his interdependences purely those having to do with the political order? "We repeat," says Dewey, "over and over that man is a social animal, and then confine the significance of this statement to the sphere in which sociality usually seems least evident, politics. The heart of the sociality of man is in education."[28]

2. The other aspect of the experiential continuum is concerned with the distinction between mind and matter. In education this distinction takes the form of physical education and instruction in the manual arts as contrasted to intellectual development. If mind and matter are utterly distinct, then the corresponding types of education have nothing to do with each other. They are separate aspects of a divided life. If life is so divided, how can the student be a unity, a whole self?

On the other hand, mentality and physicality are easily distinguishable. My thoughts have one kind of existence, my muscles and my dexterity have another. Somehow the gulf between matter and mind must be bridged, and the problem cannot be solved by reducing the one to the other. Dewey's

[28] *Reconstruction in Philosophy*, p. 185.

solution is vast in its application. It pervades his philosophy, underwriting the problem of the self and society and the problem of mind and the physical world.[29]

The error in mind-body problems comes in the starting point. Mind and matter, self and society, must be separated for many practical purposes. But in the realities of experience we never find them disconnected. Experience is not a name primarily for what happens to some thing or some person; it is the name for the reality from which the individual emerges, distinguishable but never detached from that society and that world which both requires him and undergirds him. The gulf between self and other is an artificiality of limited use. This is the way Dewey puts it:

> Experience when it happens has the same dependence upon objective natural events, physical and social, as has the occurrence of a house. It has its own objective and definitive traits; these can be described without reference to a self, precisely as a house is of brick, has eight rooms, etc., irrespective of whom it belongs to. Nevertheless, just as for some purposes and with respect to some consequences, it is all important to note the added qualification of personal ownership of real property, so with "experience." In first instance and intent, it is not exact nor relevant to say "I experience" or "I think." "It" experiences or is experienced, "it" thinks or is thought, is a juster phrase. Experience, a serial course of affairs with their own characteristic properties and relationships, occurs, happens, and is what it is. Among and within these occurrences, not outside of them nor underlying them, are those events which are denominated selves.[30]

It is important to notice that there are two types of continuity present in the continuity of experience: (a) At any given time the various aspects of experience are interconnected, and (b) throughout time experience is continuous, as a "serial course of affairs." The general outcome of this view of ex-

---

[29] Dewey expressly identifies these two as aspects of the same problem; see *Democracy and Education*, pp. 342 and 356.

[30] *Experience and Nature* (Chicago, Open Court, 1926), p. 232.

perience as being the very basic stuff of the world from which all else emerges means that any intellectual separation of the items of experience must be justified as useful or else discarded. I separate myself from the table for excellent reasons. I feed myself, not the table. I polish the table, not myself, and so on. On the plane my luggage and I dwell separately, but we jointly contribute to the load the plane must carry. These practical separations have a limited range. If I attempt to conceive of myself and the table as separate in every way, then, by definition, knowledge of the table becomes impossible.

There is a general warning contained in Dewey's doctrine of experience. The world abounds in separations which have been overdone, which ignore the basic character of the experiential continuum. Thus are separated school and society, child and curriculum, method and subject matter, to name a few with immediate educational significance.[31] The separations are useful, even vital, but imply no final disconnection. Society requires the school and the school requires society; the child is of the curriculum, and the curriculum is for the child. Method is method for some subject matter; subject matter, conversely, is methodically introduced or not at all.[32] Colleges of education, for instance, that overburden with method at the expense of subject matter might well pause at Dewey's injunction: ". . . an alleged science of methods of the mind in learning, is futile; — a mere screen for concealing the necessity a teacher is under of profound and accurate acquaintance with the subject in hand."[33]

Within the flow of experience which Dewey calls the experiential continuum there are two types of process which are especially significant for philosophy of education. They are the knowing process and the evolutionary process.

[31] *The School and Society, The Child and the Curriculum,* etc.
[32] See Nathaniel Lawrence, "Education as Social Process," in *Dewey and the Experimental Spirit in Philosophy* (ed. Charles W. Hendel, New York, Liberal Arts Press, 1959), pp. 41–49.
[33] *Democracy and Education,* p. 194.

IV

EVOLUTIONARY PROCESSES AND KNOWING PROCESSES

The continuity of the knowing self with the known world, and the continuity of the evolved human being with the evolution which is embodied in him are intimately interconnected. Not to recognize the relation of these two continuities is to be largely innocent of Dewey's educational philosophy. Dewey is explicit on these matters:

A belief in organic evolution which does not extend unreservedly to the way in which the subject of experience is thought of, and which does not strive to bring the entire theory of experience and knowing into line with biological and social facts, is hardly more than Pickwickian. . . .

If biological development be accepted, the subject of experience is at least an animal, continuous with other organic forms in a process of more complex organization. An animal in turn is at least continuous with chemico-physical processes which, in living things, are so organized as really to constitute the activities of life with all their defining traits.[34]

Race and individual have evolved in a way that lays a clear mandate on education. Meaningful education, like the biological processes which mature the merely human animal, must take the developing human being through a recapitulation of the stages through which the experience of his race has developed its own intelligence. The continuity of race experience is the presupposition of the educational curriculum:

On the face of it, the various studies, arithmetic, geography, language, botany, etc., are themselves experience — they are that of the race. They embody the cumulative outcome of the efforts, the strivings, and the successes of the human race generation after generation.[35]

[34] "The Need for a Recovery of Philosophy," in *Creative Intelligence, Essays in the Pragmatic Attitude*, by John Dewey and others (New York, Holt, 1917), pp. 35 and 36. Reprinted by permission of Holt, Rinehart and Winston, Inc.

[35] *Child and Curriculum*, p. 12.

Such race experience is the child's heritage, but it must be rediscovered *in skeletal outline* in his own experience. It cannot be plastered on him in a carefully prepared adult order.

> ... development is a definite process, having its own law which can be fulfilled only when adequate and normal conditions are provided. Really to interpret the child's present crude impulses in counting, measuring and arranging things in rhythmic series involves mathematical scholarship — a knowledge of the mathematical formulae and relations which have, in the history of the race, grown out of just such crude beginnings.[36]

If we take this idea of recapitulation in its "cultural" form, however, Dewey does not subscribe to it. Cultural recapitulation would have the child going through a savage, predatory stage, then a pastoral stage, and so on. The basic idea underlying this theory "looks primarily to the past and especially to the literary products of the past. . . ."[37] The orientation of such a theory is wrong, being directed to the past for the past's sake. It is also mistaken in its use of biological recapitulation as a model, since "Development, in short, has taken place by the entrance of short-cuts and alterations in the prior scheme of growth. And this suggests that the aim of education is to facilitate such short-circuited growth."[38]

Dewey draws a great lesson from evolution. He does not propose, however, to let that doctrine, as it is ordinarily propounded in the biology classroom, treat human beings primarily as animals whose evolution is to be understood in terms of body structure, cranial capacity, and musculature. Evolution, so conceived, is incapable of distinguishing the men of 10,000 B.C. from modern men, in any serious way. Evolutionary theory is conventionally linked with embryology in a compact formula: Ontogeny (the development of the individual) recapitulates phylogeny (the development of the species). The biological embryo passes from a blastular multicelled ball to a wormlike blob to a wormlike chordate. Early in its career it has gill slits, later a caudal appendage like a tail, and so on. The

[36] *Ibid.*, p. 17.
[37] *Democracy and Education*, p. 85. The interested student should read the general context, pp. 84–89.
[38] *Ibid.*

butterfly is a worm before it is a true insect. This is the rule of evolution: recapitulation. Embryological development retraces the history of the species.

Before the appearance of intelligence, the representative stages of recapitulation proceed by largely automatic, preset, physiological processes inherent in the fertilized ovum. But the nine-month embryo that is brought to life beyond the mother's body is rivaled only by the marsupials for underdevelopment. Even the later stages of its physiological development require a conscious environment in which to mature. Were it not for its protective society, the pitiful ex-embryo would not survive. As the infant develops, the conscious influences which call forth his own consciousness ever increase in duration, significance, and complexity. Education has begun. Before long the bringing of the resources of civilization to the child and satisfying his demand for development must pass into expert hands. This is the sure sign of a civilization, whether it be found in the palace tutor or in the roadside school: the civilization is just as good as the continuous and conscious effort at education which surrounds the maturing of its leadership-to-be.

In the development of the race from which men have emerged and by which they are still evolving there are stored untold thousands of years of experience. Education must select those features of experience which lie along the main line of growth — those which have been most productive of further growth — and bring them, in essence, to the developing human being. In doing so it runs the risk of abstraction.

We abstract what is significant and basic from what is relatively trivial or dependent. Even if we put aside the question of how to be sure that we are condensing the prime achievements of our race into our curriculum — and the question is not easy to answer — we must face the fact that the process tends to be one more of isolation than of condensation. Take the classic example of geometry. The Egyptians had a good working geometry. It was empirical wisdom gained over a long period of time. They had the 3-4-5 triangle, but they did not know it as a special case of what we call the Pythagorean theorem. This know-how geometry was tied up with the sociology, the climate, the religion, and the geology of the time and place. All these factors, for instance, are interrelated in the building of the great pyramids. With the rise of Greek philosophy, geometry rapidly matured into a formal science of scope, certainty, and power, largely freed from its dependence on observation and experiment. But it was built upon hundreds of years of steady, accumulating, human experience. The monument of Euclidean geometry stood, as an unquestioned formal discipline with extraordinary breadth of application, for two thousand years. We teach geometry as Euclid saw it, detached from its origins in practical art and its interconnection with culture. It suddenly appears in the conventional curriculum, dazzling and perfect, in the junior year of high school. It is a model of rigorous reasoning. It gets farfetched results, which are nevertheless unassailable, for it begins with what no one challenges and proceeds to its conclusion by faultless logic. Probably all who suffer its regimen are better men and women. But what a waste!

How often is the student shown that the Greek strategies of war depended on this same spatial sense, which is as old as those curious things, the figures in the constellations? Would it occur to you that the constellations are really figures of men and animals? The same spatial sense is crystallized in the golden age of Greek architecture.[39] In our haste to get geometry into the student's mind as soon as his power of abstraction will permit, we largely isolate geometry from its natural origins and let it run its full course into theorems of challenging complexity and virtually no known application. Only the sense of abstract beauty, elegance, and rigor remains to excite our interest.

Recently some of the isolation has been broken down by introducing geometry through the elementary algebraic techniques of analytic geometry. The method is anachronistic, but it serves at least to bridge the moat around geometry. Other cross-disciplinary efforts of a similar nature have appeared. The problem is, however, a twofold one. Not only are our "subjects" taught isolated and abstracted from one another — this difficulty the cross-disciplinary study assaults with con-

[39] But the Greeks developed no facile arithmetical techniques, and therefore no algebra and thus no machines of any complexity and no celestial dynamics of mathematical depth, till the Alexandrian period.

siderable success — but they are abstracted from the need, the problems, the challenge that gave rise to them in the first place. The theme is basic in Dewey's philosophy of education. The race did not simply go out and get knowledge because someone thought it would be a good idea, nor because it was a prevailing social habit. However well Aristotle's "All men by nature desire to know" may express the inner challenge of concrete problems and problematic situations which provide the specific targets for the desire, "The function of reflective thought is, therefore, to transform a situation in which there is experienced obscurity, doubt, conflict, disturbance of some sort, into a situation that is clear, coherent, settled, harmonious."[40] The more we are tempted to settle for the "speediest return into the world where one can act,"[41] the more swiftly a new doubt will appear, the natural outcome of our limited sense of what is practical. Thought will be challenged again, and the process starts over.[42]

This approach to the problem of thought is pervasive throughout Dewey's philosophy, whether or not it has direct bearing on educational theory and practice. Dewey calls it "experimental logic," meaning to emphasize the logic of experiment in which thought must engage when it is confronted with a problematic situation.[43] He also calls this approach an "instrumentalism," to indicate that thought is not a detached process imposed upon or derived from the natural world but an instrument in the natural world whereby a problem that blocks some intent or purpose is resolved. The old problem of the separation between thought and thing, mind and body, Dewey regards as illusory. Experience never reveals detached pure thought, or objects disconnected from thinking processes.[44]

[40] *How We Think* (Boston, Heath, rev. ed., 1933), as reprinted in Joseph Ratner, ed., *Intelligence in the Modern World: John Dewey's Philosophy* (New York, Random House, 1939), p. 851.

[41] *Essays in Experimental Logic* (Chicago, University of Chicago Press, 1916, and New York, Dover Publications, n.d.), p. 184.

[42] The process really follows four phases: belief, doubt, reflection, and empirical inference. The interested reader should consult *Essays in Experimental Logic*, pp. 183–216.

[43] See *ibid.*, esp. the Introduction.

[44] *Ibid.*, pp. 30, 31, 35, and 75–102.

Since thought always proceeds by way of unraveling some doubt or solving some problem, and knowledge is the outcome of thought, to present the knowledge without the problems that it arose to meet is to ask the student to shake hands with a scarecrow. Obviously each child cannot crawl up the millions of rungs in the ladder by which his race has ascended, but for him to be utterly divorced from the reasonableness for knowing what we expect him to know is not only to deny him his race heritage but to inculcate an early suspicion of education. The worth of education cannot rest in a set of promissory notes, to be redeemed when the student reaches maturity. This is the reason why Dewey insists that learning cannot be dissociated from activity. He is not suggesting that mechanical skills be substituted for genuine intellectual development. He is insisting that contact with representative — and perhaps necessarily simplified — concrete problems provides the student with a reasonableness for his endeavor. It helps him to recover in skeletal outline the struggle of his race for the knowledge it has won. Equally important, it gives him early practice in the art of inquiring, which will serve him well when the period of formal training is over.

Of course, the doubts and the problems which thinking is intended to solve may be at some remove from tangible action. But such problems and their solving are of an extremely sophisticated sort, only lately engaged in by our race. They necessarily come late in the child's development also. When we ignore this fact we are trying to get him to run and swim before he can walk or float. Like Rousseau, Dewey is warning us to learn from nature what the natural mode of learning is. Its graded steps follow a natural order. The difference lies, of course, in the conception of nature.

Much fun has been made of Dewey's views on the need for an action-grounded knowledge, particularly since it is on this subject that he is most sympathetic with the progressivists.[45] But educators should take solemn note of the correlation be-

[45] See, for instance, the scintillating satirical story "The Schartz-Metterklume Method," by Saki (H. H. Munro) and the progressive school episode in Patrick Dennis' *Auntie Mame* (New York, Vanguard, 1954).

tween the increasingly abstract character of education at all levels and the increased boredom of students. Boredom is a major problem in high school education; it is a major contributor to the collegiate "sophomore slump." In the experience of the authors of this book an overwhelming number of students who flunk out or leave college for a year or more to engage in more tangible occupations, *if they return,* come back with a seriousness and purposiveness which is astonishing. It will do no good for educators to point to a vague social materialism, the breakdown of the family system, international tension, and so on, as the cause of the failure of education to attract and hold the students' interests. Either education plays a substantial role in shaping persons or it does not. To the extent that it does, it must accept substantial responsibility for the student disaffection with education. It cannot avoid the demand that its resources be useful resources.

It is clear that the major hazards occur early, when the child's education is giving him his first knowledge and his first tools and when his patterns of motivation are being established. The crucial problem is to be sure that his natural eagerness to learn is not squashed by the imposition of — to him — meaningless ends. We stress quick performance in the acquiring of basic intellectual skills which, if more slowly acquired, might be both more reasonable and more satisfying. The use of flash cards in the teaching of reading, for instance, one such performance-valued technique, is now markedly on the wane. Its weaknesses are manifest.

The knowing process thus cannot be torn away from the other processes of which it is a part, particularly the social process and the evolutionary process. They bear on it as it does on them. The "experiential continuum" is inclusive of them all. It is *not* the case that "experience as such is primarily cognitional — a knowledge affair." Rather, it "is always a matter of the use that is made of experienced natural events. . . ."[46] This is true not only of the young child, to whom it strongly applies, but also of most adults.

"All people," writes Dewey, "at the outset, and the majority of people probably all their lives, attain to some ordering of

[46] "Need for a Recovery of Philosophy," p. 47; see also pp. 36–37.

thought through ordering of action."[47] "The two principles of continuity and interaction are not separate from each
other."[48] The primary ordering of life lies in the ordering of
action. Ordered thought is the outcome of such action. Only
at a relatively high level of education can ordered thought
proceed with its umbilical cord cut. The young child begins
by manipulating coordinately in short spans long before it
plans or articulates its thought in language. The passage from
root action to pure thought is gradual. The great fallacy in the
old traditional education lies in the supposition that language,
early mathematics, history, and all the rest can be learned
devoid of the action-meanings which they have. If there be no
maturity of experience, the capacity to memorize, to learn by
rote, and to anticipate test-response situations can be forcibly
developed, but it is wanting in any educational value. If it
comes to have educational value late, it will be in spite of such
an educational system, not because of it.

V

EDUCATION AND THE HUMAN SELF

It is clear that the doctrine of evolution is for Dewey a
genuine account of the way the world goes, not just a con-
venient explanatory device which accommodates the geological
and embryological data.

What Dewey does is not to model the psychic life on physiological life but to extend the significance of evolution into the
distinctively human. The shape of human characteristics depends on the more or less conscious efforts of educators, which
efforts must be self-conscious and self-critical. This is the
reason Dewey emphasized method so strongly, not because he
thought that subject matter could be profitably minimized.

It is not the case that a curriculum should be constantly
under revision. It should be under a constant scrutiny and
review. Moreover, the transmission of all learning is not its
task.

[47] *How We Think*, in Ratner, pp. 615–616.
[48] *Experience and Education*, p. 42.

The first office of the social organ we call the school is to provide a *simplified* environment. . . . It establishes a purified medium of action. . . . As a society becomes more enlightened, it realizes that it is responsible *not* to transmit and conserve the whole of its existing achievements, but only such as make for a better future society.[49]

It is tempting to ask Dewey for a set of rules to judge what will make for a better future society. We are then only asking for a new dogma instead of an old one. "We educate," says Dewey in criticism of education, "for a static social order which does not exist."[50] Not only does the experimental spirit in human development uncover new means to old ends, but it discovers new ends, and these cannot be assessed until they are at least envisaged. Consider such contemporary occupations as international economic development, computer logistics, city planning, industrial research, to mention only a few. None of these would have made even verbal sense in Lincoln's day a century ago. Each of them has a social role; each offers a mode of individual self-realization. As a result, each makes a claim on the educational system from which it draws its personnel. There can be no eternally good curriculum.

We shall investigate the relation between self and society in the following section. At this point we ask, "What is the self?" The core of self, for Dewey, is not intelligence or rationality, nor is it desire or appetite, nor even, primarily, responsive sensitivity. The core is will, and will is scarcely distinguishable from the totality of habit. Dewey says habits are "demands for certain kinds of activity" that constitute the self and that in "any intelligible sense of the word will, they *are* will."[51] This is a giant equation: habit, will, self, — and it needs commentary.

The term "habit" in Dewey is elusive, and delusive. Its scope is almost as broad as that of "experience." To say that habits collectively constitute the self and then to say, as Dewey does, that "Habits as organized activities are secondary and acquired, not native and original,"[52] amounts to telling us that the self is secondary and acquired, being merely a set of "outgrowths of unlearned activities which are part of man's en-

[49] *Democracy and Education*, p. 24.
[50] *Education and the Social Order*, p. 9.
[51] *Human Nature and Conduct*, p. 25.   [52] *Ibid.*, p. 89.

dowment at birth."[53] And this is exactly what Dewey means to say. The self *is* an outgrowth of unlearned activities; they are prior to its emergence; it *is* a secondary development. That is what education in the broad sense is for — to assist in the birth of a self from the "unlearned activities" which are its native endowment. It is for this reason that freedom, as we saw earlier, is not an "original possession," but "something to be achieved, to be wrought out." When there is no self there is no freedom, and the converse is also true: no freedom, no self.

It should be clear that in this simple scheme something is missing, however. On the one hand, there are natural activities; on the other, there are habits, collectively equated with the will and the self. What else is primary, on a par with the natural activities that would urge a developing human being to be self-creating from its background of natural activities? Dewey calls it "impulse."

"Impulse is primary and intelligence is secondary and in some sense derivative."[54] "Impulse" is often used interchangeably with "instinct."[55] Unfortunately, "impulse" suggests utter whimsicality and "instinct" suggests an unalterable drive. Either term is therefore somewhat misleading. What Dewey is describing is indeed a thing blind,[56] but it is neither as completely chaotic as "impulse" in the ordinary sense nor as inaccessible to intelligence as "instinct."[57] Dewey refers to man's seething, undirected, but directable tendencies under the title of "instinct" in the second motto of this essay. There is always a superabundance of them. Education, in the broad sense that includes the total effect of the environment, aids in the selection, organization, and patterning of these creative capacities. Their creative role is clear: "Impulses are the pivots upon which the re-organization of activities turn, they are agencies of deviation, for giving new directions to old habits and changing their quality."[58] The organized impulse which becomes a habit is an interest,[59] which is the true basis of

[53] *Ibid.*
[56] *Ibid.*, p. 254.
[59] *Ibid.*, p. 164.

[54] *Ibid.*, p. 254.
[57] *Ibid.*

[55] *Ibid.*, p. 105 n.
[58] *Ibid.*, p. 93.

intelligence. Intelligence is indeed secondary, derivative, but this does not mean that it is a "slave of impulse." On the contrary, intelligence aims to clarify and liberate impulse from its tanglefoot ways.[60]

Habits are the citadels of order and routine. Impulse is the fountain of imagination, "tumultuous and confused."[61] Habit involves repetition and mechanization at its base, but there must be an infusion of more than mechanization.[62] In this mechanization lies the "force of habit" which Dewey regards as usually "a stronger and deeper part of human nature than is desire for change."[63] For this reason true intelligence requires a growing tip of new interest, lest it fall back into routine habit.

What does all this come to? Surely not a didactic or precise picture. Dewey's spirited attack on the complacencies of an older tradition cannot be followed by a clear-cut substitute. He is telling us how to look, not explaining exactly what we will see. The child arrives in the world with minimal routine habits in company with a superabundance of impulse, in need of organization toward the goals of freedom and selfhood. As a consequence, he needs supervision, guidance, control. But these must not be the imposition of a settled adult pattern, abstractly distilled and served up in uniform small pieces, a bit at a time. Rather the guidance functions are directed toward a native impulse and a native — but minimal — set of habits, with a view to fusing the two into a genuine self, and this means taking the natural forms of activity, manual, manipulative, and the like, through the stages of development which they have actually played in the evolution of the race. Failure to provide a graded realization of the race inheritance robs the person of his birthright and thereby minimizes the benefit society will receive from him. We are thus faced with our final topic: the self and society.

[60] *Ibid.*, p. 255.
[61] *Ibid.*, p. 177.
[62] *Ibid.*, p. 70.
[63] "Authority and Social Change," from *Authority and the Individual,* Harvard Tercentenary Conference of the Arts and Sciences (Cambridge, Harvard University Press, 1937), in Ratner, *op. cit.*, p. 348.

VI

The Self and Society

Dewey is consistently suspicious of dichotomies like "school and society," "child and curriculum," "progressive and conservative education." His aim is to show that theory requires the intercommitment of the two in every case.

Much license and much laziness disguised as "permissiveness" have been laid at Dewey's door. If anything, Dewey emphasizes the social demands and values of education. His reasons for such emphasis are not based on political conviction, nor are they even primarily sociological. They lie at the very basis of his total philosophy. ". . . All human experience is ultimately social."[64] "Experience does not go on simply inside a person."[65] Experience of course has its subjective side, but to the extent that we emphasize this private viewpoint we are unable to explain its public impact. One of the silly consequences of such a de-emphasizing of the public side of experience is that we have no way of explaining the transition from savagery to civilization which the race has accomplished. The truth of the matter is that "we live from birth to death in a world of persons and things which in large measure is what it is because of what has been done and transmitted from previous human activities."[66] ". . . Intellectual organization is not an end in itself but is the means by which social relations, distinctively human ties and bonds, may be understood and more intelligently ordered."[67]

Over against the *social* aspects of *knowledge* is clearly the *individual* basis of human *thought*. "The phrase 'think for one's self' is a pleonasm. Unless one does it for one's self, it isn't thinking. . . . Thinking is as much an individual matter as is the digestion of food."[68] It is important to recognize that thinking is not simply a right or a privilege of individuals, on the one hand, nor is it merely in the nature of things that there

[64] *Experience and Education*, p. 32.
[65] *Ibid.*, p. 33. [66] *Ibid.*, p. 34. [67] *Ibid.*, p. 103.
[68] *Democracy and Education*, p. 353.

is no corporate thinking, on the other. Society itself requires these private sources of thought with their possible public benefits. The public risk of a disruption of settled patterns must be accepted. "A progressive society counts individual variations as precious since it finds in them the means of its own growth. Hence a democratic society must, in consistency with its ideal, allow for intellectual freedom and the play of diverse gifts and interests in its educational measures."[69]

To one form of individualism Dewey is unequivocally opposed. He insists that we must substitute "social purpose," requiring a control of the "teaching and discipline and materials of study, for the traditional individualistic aim."[70] Through such substitution there will come to be "more genuine development of individuality for the mass of individuals."[71] The individualism to which Dewey refers is, however, not an independence of mind but an economic individualism. "The common faith," he says, in speaking of this concept, "was the cult of individual success by means of individual effort."[72] This cult arose in the pioneer and frontier phases of the American democracy, but it survived the conversion of the United States to an industrial democracy. In its still primitive form it has flourished and grown, extending into all classes and groups[73] and driving men apart from their common cause and mutual dependence.

Dewey here strikes at the heart of a major American ailment, perhaps *the* major American ailment. Our political conception of liberty has become a negative conception of freedom that readily generates an attitude of "I'll get mine first." Dewey's protests anticipate the present era of pressure politics by pressure groups formed on the basis of their special interests, rather than from an understanding of their common need. Full education results, for Dewey, in sharing in the aims and policies of the social groups to which one belongs. Democracy is not something consecrated by government sanction. It is, he says,

but a name for the fact that human nature is developed only when its elements take part in directing things which are com-

[69] *Ibid.*, p. 357.   [70] *Education and the Social Order*, p. 8.
[71] *Ibid.*   [72] *Ibid.*, p. 6.   [73] *Ibid.*, p. 7.

mon, things for the sake of which men and women form groups — families, industrial companies, governments, churches, scientific associations and so on. The principle holds as much of one form of association, say in industry and commerce, as it does in government. The identification of democracy with political democracy which is responsible for most of its failures is, however, based upon the traditional ideas which make the individual and the state ready-made entities in themselves.[74]

Moreover, "social dependencies and interdependencies are as important for the adult as for the child."[75]

What are we to say, then, of the relation between the self and society as it shapes the curriculum, its disciplines, and its methods? The problem takes shape at the level of action. "There is no inherent opposition between *working with* others and *working as* an individual."[76] Notice the words "with" and "as." Dewey's early educational theory stressed group activity and was therefore mistakenly identified with the permissive play approach to education. As manual activity proceeds through tool manipulation toward more and more sustained uses of imagination, memory, inquiry, and abstraction, however, the intellective element strengthens. The individual person is emerging.

Where intellect becomes an important factor, the question of independence and interdependence becomes acute. The human intellect is actualized only gradually. First a group of rudimentary habitual activities, physiologically embodied and oriented, become a *self* through a progress in types of habit. Secondly, the self gradually develops a mental status. "The self *achieves* mind in the degree in which knowledge of things is incarnate in the life about him; the self is not a separate mind building up knowledge anew on its own account."[77]

Mind is thus a second-order derivative. Primary, virtually automatic habits underlie the emergent self. The self in turn achieves a mind, a self-created thing relying upon the knowledge embedded in the self's own social matrix. Knowledge, as

[74] *Reconstruction in Philosophy*, pp. 209–210.
[75] *Ibid.*, p. 185.
[76] *Democracy and Education*, p. 353; italics ours.
[77] *Ibid.*, p. 344.

Dewey speaks of it, is public property, or at least public presumption. Everything is called knowledge "which is taken for granted in our intercourse with one another and nature. . . ."[78] "Thinking on the contrary, starts, as we have seen, from doubt or uncertainty."[79] Thinking is that through which knowledge is revised, and it is subjective and personal.[80] "Unless one does it for one's self it isn't thinking."

The lesson for education is perfectly clear. The subjectivity of thinking, through which alone the otherwise dead (and sometimes mistaken) knowledge of the race becomes meaningful, requires a recapitulation of the high points in the development of human understanding. The objectivity of the race's knowledge is thus under constant question-by-review. The knowledge thus encountered is also alive, in whatever measure the subjective processes of thinking, building upon it, creatively add to it.

The socio-political lesson too becomes plain. Let the individual be warned: The immense heritage that is his is so by reason of a corporate effort in which his own human status is embedded; this is especially true of the knowledge which gives to his self, under his special form of ingestion, a mentality. Let society be warned as well: All knowledge arises from and is tested by the subjective and individual functions of thinking. Society alters when it clamps down on what may or must be studied; society is itself a low-grade organism, possessing inherent knowledge but no capacity to think. Thinking is a vital and individual enterprise. The final word on this matter is the watchword of genuine freedom in a corporate and interdependent society: "Regarding freedom, the important thing to bear in mind is that it designates a mental attitude *rather than external unconstraint of movements,* but that this quality of mind cannot develop without a fair leeway of movements in exploration, experimentation, application, etc."[81] The era of the wholly self-determining man never existed. In the period of America's expanding frontier it came closest to its nearly chaotic realization. Freedom is, however, a vital part of all life, social and individual, and it lives in the essential quality of

[78] *Ibid.,* p. 345.   [79] *Ibid.*   [80] *Ibid., passim.*
[81] *Ibid.,* p. 357; italics ours.

man, his capacity to think, and thereby to enrich both society and himself.

Suggestions for Further Reading

Dewey's most detailed work on education is *Democracy and Education* (New York, Macmillan, 1916). Of his many provocative essays on the subject, the two selected by Leonard Carmichael in *The Child and the Curriculum and The School and Society* (Chicago, University of Chicago Press, 1956) have been generously used in our essay and should be read in their entirety. Students who want to pursue Dewey's thinking on special educational subjects are referred to *A Cyclopedia of Education* (ed. Paul Monroe, 5 vols., New York, Macmillan, 1911–1913). Over one hundred of the articles are by Dewey.

Probably the best single introduction to Dewey's work in general is the Modern Library *Intelligence in the Modern World: John Dewey's Philosophy* (ed. Joseph Ratner, New York, Random House, 1939). Ratner's introduction to the volume is a book in itself. It lacks grace and order, but it is saturated with the Deweyan spirit, and the coverage is extremely good. The selections from Dewey extend to better than eight hundred pages, again with excellent coverage, but marred by Ratner's unhappy habit of cutting and pasting, without indication, of sometimes widely separated texts. Nothing should be cited or seriously digested from this volume without being back-checked to its source. Readers with less interest or time may read Richard Bernstein's informative and instructive introduction to his *John Dewey on Experience, Nature, and Freedom* (New York, Liberal Arts Press, 1960). The essays reprinted in this volume are generally broad in their coverage but do not include anything on education. For complete bibliography the authoritative source is *John Dewey, a Centennial Bibliography*, by Milton Halsey Thomas (Chicago, University of Chicago Press, 1962), which requires 153 pages to list the titles of all Dewey's writings.

The Philosophy of John Dewey (ed. Paul Arthur Schilpp, Vol. I of the Library of Living Philosophers, Evanston, Northwestern University Press, 1939) includes essays by John L. Childs ("The Educational Philosophy of John Dewey") and William H. Kilpatrick ("Dewey's Influence on Education"), which are complementary in method and content and jointly provide a good survey of Dewey's educational thought from the side of the devoted professional. A shorter essay, emphasizing a small number of points, is Nathaniel Lawrence, "Education as Social Process," in C. W. Hendel, ed., *John Dewey and the Experimental Spirit in Philosophy* (New York, Liberal Arts Press, 1959). For those who wish to read further on Dewey's educational theory, we recommend the entries under Childs and Kilpatrick in Thomas's *Bibliography,* cited above.

CHAPTER SEVEN

Whitehead: *The Rhythm of Nature*

I

THREE NATURALISMS

Whitehead is one of the three great modern philosophers of education. The other two are Dewey and Rousseau. All are concerned with the relation between nature and man, and all are concerned with man's development, individually and socially.

Rousseau came to philosophy of education by way of social theory. Disgusted with the artificialities of royal courts and the pursuit of luxuries in the cities, he regarded civilization as a departure from nature. How then to educate the good citizen? Since civilization corrupts, education cannot aim primarily at civilizing. Good education trains the young to resist society and its evils. Raise Émile in the country, where pastoral people in small, face-to-face communities are also face to face with nature. Let him live close to nature and learn by simple, direct means what men have learned before. If he breaks a window, neither scold him nor replace it for him. Let him be exposed to the weather, and the importance of windows will be experienced, not lectured on. The emphasis on experience, rather than on authority or formal reasoning, marks the transition to the modern period. Here, in Rousseau's romance of the individual, and without the theory of organic evolution, we find a simple insistence that in education the individual repeats the experience of the race. Nature for Rousseau was thus something to be lived with, to be learned from, and to be nourished by. Ultimately nature herself was conceived in typical eighteenth-century terms, a world of scientific laws which are the laws of mechanics, terrestrial and celestial, established by God and revealed by the genius of Isaac Newton. Yet nature was also romanticized as the great teacher of the virtues of simplicity, honesty, and directness. To live close to nature was to live well.

Rousseau's naturalism is a blend of romantic and mechanistic naturalism. Dewey's naturalism, however, is evolutionary. There is a marked contrast. Newton had taught that in the machinery of nature things were always done in the simplest way. Bodies fall in straight lines unless other forces intervene; they stay at rest or in uniform motion unless externally interfered with. The world is ultimately made up of simple particles, pure space, and pure time. The post-Newtonian world, as a result, took it for granted that the behavior of all things physical could finally be reduced to the immutable laws of mechanics and the immutable things with which they dealt: space, time, and matter. With the advent of Darwin, the shape of science changed substantially. The nineteenth-century revolution in science came in the theory of *living* beings. Let matter be as it may, here is life. How is it organized? Where does the great diversity of species come from? How about all those animals and plants known only from fossil remains? Where do they fit in? Is there an obscure divine scheme for creation — "How unsearchable are his ways, and his judgments past finding out" — or could one discover the sense in things by observation and thought? With Darwin the problem of the diversity of species, living and dead, and the presence of man in nature produced a scientific theory unlike previous scientific laws. This theory placed man squarely in nature as a complex animal evolved from simpler forms, as they had evolved from still simpler forms.

After Darwin, to look for simplicity is to look not for ultimates but for ancestors. But these forms have evolved in a giant struggle for survival, in which chance variations in species either help or hinder that survival. Nature is no Newtonian machine endlessly operating according to the laws of mechanics. The machine metaphor is inadequate to the dynamic emergence of species. Instead we have the metaphors of the battlefield, the open competitive economic market, and even the gaming table. The stakes are life and death of the species itself.

Under the metaphors of competition and struggle also we must place Dewey's emphasis on knowledge as coming from the resolving of a tension. Humanity learns when it is placed in a problem situation requiring solution. The child learns the *method* of learning by being given problem-solving tasks. Moreover, since men have emerged from lower forms, human society is not in opposition to nature but rather an outgrowth of nature. Dewey thus recaptures the Aristotelian insight that the social condition is natural to man and couples it with the evolutionary doctrine that complex forms (in this case societies) arise from simpler ones and do so naturally. Dewey's educational naturalism, then, is an education for society, not in spite of society or for the sake of resisting its urban forms. Dewey, with Rousseau, wants men to live according to nature, but he conceives nature as including the complex society rather than being corrupted by it, evolving rather than remaining the same, tending toward complexity rather than simplicity. Intelligence is man's great device for adaptation. The cultivation of intelligence is essential in man's struggle to survive in nature and to overcome the self-created internal problems of his own increasingly complex society. Dewey's naturalism is evolutionary and pragmatic. It exploits the idea of the evolution, growth, and development of human society. It insists on the practical control and nourishment of this growth by concrete encounter on the part of the student with the living problems which his race has met and mastered. Thereby the student gains knowledge.

As Rousseau comes to philosophy by way of an interest in social theory, and Dewey by way of biology and psychology, so Whitehead, also a naturalist, comes by way of mathematics and physics, which, not surprisingly, are included in his view of nature.

Rousseau's eighteenth-century naturalism was strongly under the sway of Newton's mechanism. The nineteenth-century revolution concentrates on man as part of a vast fauna with whom he is in intimate kinship. But physics has hardly died in the meantime, and late in the nineteenth century the work that was to mature into Relativity theory was undertaken. The twentieth century was dominated by that theory. Whitehead takes from the Darwinian theory, as does Dewey, the conception of organic evolution. In fact, he calls his philosophy the philosophy of organism. But he further asks himself, If the theory of Relativity is true of nature and man is within nature, what sort of relations must hold between man and the rest of nature? No doubt the post-Newtonian mechanism of the eighteenth century was naïve. But it was a clearheaded century in one way: It believed in consistency. If nature is a machine and man is wholly in nature, then man is a machine too. Indeed, fourteen years before Rousseau published *Émile*, Julien de La Mettrie, court adviser to Frederick the Great ("court atheist," Voltaire called him) published a work called *L'Homme Machine*, in which he portrayed men as highly complex machines.

From Darwin Whitehead draws the recognition of the basically organic character of the natural scene. But from the eighteenth century he draws the conviction that if a scientific theory is true, it is significant not merely for nature in general but also for men in particular, who are parts of nature. As Whitehead says in his remarks on the eighteenth century:[1] ". . . we can hope to see that it is necessary that there should be an *order* of nature."[2] Dewey's view of human nature and its education is shaped by the theory of evolution. The same is true for Whitehead, but in addition Whitehead's view of human nature and its education is shaped by the theory of Relativity. If we take no account of this fact, we can only

[1] *Science and the Modern World* (New York, Macmillan, and London, Cambridge University Press, 1925, and New American Library of World Literature, 1948), chap. IV. Throughout this chapter page references to paperback reprints, where they are different from the originals, will be given second, in brackets.

[2] *Ibid.,* p. 108 [75]; italics ours.

see a Whiteheadean technology of education, not a philosophy of education.

II

WHITEHEAD AND RELATIVITY

The importance of Relativity theory for Whitehead lies principally in the following considerations: Newton had separated space, time, and matter from one another. Matter was thus the machinery, and space and time were the where and when in which the machinery operated. These simplifications permitted a mathematical view of the world having enormous scope and power, but they had an intrinsic limitation: No one had ever encountered pure space or pure time, and the pursuit of pure matter was soon to reveal it as electromagnetic disturbances rather than as just little bits of stuff. This limitation came to light when experiments intended to measure great spaces and velocities through the spaces produced paradoxical results.[3] There is no such thing as pure space and pure time; rather, spatiality and temporality are features of events and processes, including those events which are the activities of the observers! The physicist finds himself having to speak of *his* state of motion or rest, relative to what he is observing or describing. His observations will be *relative* to such motion. He cannot give them in any absolute way, but only in relation to the system which he observes. The factors of time, space, and motion are thus interdependent, not independent, and are functions of one another. Their reality depends on that of the processes, the series of events which are spatially and temporally extended, not vice versa, as in Newton. Furthermore, the investigation of the fine structure of matter presented something of the same picture. The electrons and protons of the earlier atomic theory now appear as electromagnetic fields of activity. Matter itself, submicroscopically, thus turns out to

[3] The classical first experiment was the Michelson-Morley experiment, which was followed by many others. This topic and related ones are discussed in nearly all popular summaries of Relativity theory.

be an intricate series of events, activities, and processes. Grossly, the table is a thing. In reality it is a vast swarm of activities, of energy in intricate balance. The theory proposes not merely to treat matter as energy, but also to regard it as such. It inaugurates the atomic age and the tapping of the trapped energy which is matter.

The generalization of Relativity theory beyond its applications to physical particles underlies the title of Whitehead's masterwork, *Process and Reality*,[4] because, for Whitehead, process *is* reality. Not only are space, time, and matter essentially interdependent, but the same interdependence is present in the world of colors, sounds, observable objects, and the like. Moreover, this world of common perception and that of the physicist must be interrelated as well. Like Dewey, Whitehead knows that a good scientific theory is not a mere scientific theory. If science has something to say about reality (and why listen, if it doesn't?), then its theories have something to do with reality as a whole. Relativity is a universal principle, not just a scientific one.

The table on which this book rests (and indeed the book itself) can be treated as a solid swarm of swirling electromagnetic fields. The brownness of the table, stable as it is, must be attributed partly to these electromagnetic processes, partly to those in our retinas, partly to the neurological processes in our nervous systems, and so on. The ingredient "brown" is indeed a steady object, as is "table," but these ingredients do not exist by themselves. In order to *be,* they must dwell or live in the complex process of events which support them. We can treat of them by themselves without reference to any processes — e.g., "Brown is a color," "Good tables are strong," and so on — but they cannot be actual except insofar as they are characteristic of some process or processes. The basic conviction here is that *all that is actual is essentially time-structured.*

Educational development is also, of course, a temporal process. As we shall see, the essential thing in education is that the process of education be composed of subordinate processes,

[4] *Process and Reality* (New York, Macmillan, 1929, and Harper Torchbooks, 1960).

appropriate to the successive phases of the developing person and each having a cyclic pattern of its own.

III

PHYSICAL EDUCATION AND INTELLECTUAL EDUCATION

Human beings are physical beings. Their lives are lived through the physical processes which make up their bodies. But human life has a mental side. Exclusive attention to the physical processes which go along with our intellectual, spiritual, moral, and social activities will not tell us much about those activities unless we already have direct acquaintance with them. For instance, a lie detector can chart my breathing, sweating, and so on, on a graph, but unless I already know directly what fear itself is like, the physical side of fear is only a bunch of meaningless lines on a graph. The fact that the mental side of life cannot be separated from the physical side does not rob mental life of its distinctive character. And the presence in human beings of this characteristic mentality poses a nice problem for anyone who takes evolutionary doctrine seriously: What did mentality emerge from? If life emerged chemically from atoms, did human thought emerge from lower life? Before Darwin, philosophers regarded God as responsible for the minds and souls of men. Now what? This was the question on which turned so much of the "warfare of science and religion" in the late nineteenth century. Any answer to these questions cannot be given casually or briefly, but putting aside questions of theology and religion, Whitehead's answer to the problem of emergent mentality is quite clear.

If human life is to be traced back to the so-called "purely physical" matter, there must have been, latent in such matter, however primitively, the "makings" of mentality at the outset. We must look for the roots of mentality in what is ordinarily thought of as simple "physical" existence. As Whitehead uses the term "mentality," it is a name for these simple beginnings. The point is of the utmost educational significance. For if education is integral to living development and the living human being recapitulates in broad outline the stages through which its remote ancestry has passed, *then the mental side of education at the outset must lie close to the physical side.* There is nothing recherché about this conclusion. Our earliest education lies at the obviously physical level: in manipulation and coordination. It proceeds gradually to imitative vocalization, which nourishes the deep roots of the capacity to think. The gradual emergence of mind from matter we thus see in the developing infant. We presume the same development of the human species generally. We are therefore led to look for the basis of mentality in what would ordinarily be regarded as the purely physical. Whitehead holds that mentality, taken in its broadest sense, is characteristic of all natural processes.

> But every occasion of experience is dipolar. It is mental experience integrated with physical experience. Mental experience is the converse of bodily experience. . . . Consciousness is no necessary element in mental experience.

> The higher forms of intellectual experience only arise when there are complex integrations, and reintegrations, of mental and physical experience.[5]

Mental development, even in the narrow sense of the word, is inescapably linked to physical development, and in an interesting way: The lower vertebrates develop into dominantly physical beings more or less automatically, during which process the main stages of their ancestral evolution are retraced. Human beings, however, develop through acculturation and education. *Educational and cultural processes shape the individual as surely as do the more innate physical factors.* Whitehead did not suppose that the physical stage of existence was simply to be passed through and thereafter lived with, while mentality went about its higher business. The physical is with us throughout our lives, rightly and importantly so. To William Ernest Hocking he wrote:

[5] Alfred North Whitehead, *The Function of Reason* (Lewis Clark Vanuxem Foundation Lectures delivered at Princeton University, March, 1929. Princeton, Princeton University Press, 1929. Copyright November 5, 1929. Reprinted in paperback by Beacon Press, Boston, 1957), pp. 25–26 [32–33].

And what is the prime character of History? Compulsion — symbolized by the traffic cop — No, this is still too intellectual — *being tackled at Rugby, there is the Real.* Nobody who hasn't been knocked down has the slightest notion of what the Real is. . . . I used to play in the middle of the scrum. They used to hack at your shins to make you surrender the ball, a compulsory element — but the question was *How you took it* — your own self-creation. Freedom lies in summoning up a mentality which transforms the situation, as against letting organic reactions take their course.[6]

If being tackled at Rugby is the Real, and freedom lies in summoning up a mentality which transforms the situation, any effort to divorce the physical and mental in education is undertaken at some peril. Unwittingly our attitudes toward physical and mental education reflect a misunderstanding of the emergence of mentality, as if minds had left bodies more or less behind in the way that sea animals deserted marine existence for dry land. As a race we delegate athletics to the young, whose natural enthusiasm wanes in a few years, or to a professional few, whose skilled antics we vicariously enjoy from the stands or on the TV screen. If we exercise as adults, we drive a few blocks to play tennis or motor-scooter from golf hole to golf hole. As for the exercise and training of manual skill, this is to be found in summer camps for children, clubs for restless housewives, and highly mechanized home shops for businessmen to escape to. In short, adult life largely excludes the physical aspects of life. It is ironic that in an era of considerable materialism there is surprisingly little attention to genuine physical education. Attention or no, the physical will out. Whitehead says in a stunning passage linking the misguided separation of mind and body with the theory of evolution:

I lay it down as an educational axiom that in teaching you will come to grief as soon as you forget that your pupils have bodies. This is exactly the mistake of the post-renaissance Platonic curriculum. But nature can be kept at bay by no pitchfork; so in English education, being expelled from the classroom, she returned with a cap and bells in the form of all-conquering athleticism.[7]

The point is clear: hand and brain reciprocally evolved. The brain materially embodies mind. Mind is materially explicit, through the hand. Mind and body are in mutual demand — and the demand cannot be too well met by an alternation between mental and physical activity. It must in some degree be met by activity which coordinates the two. Better that the intellectual attend to creative writing and speaking as physical balance to his reading than that he satisfy himself by small admixtures of tennis and gardening.

In physical education the question is not, When do we abandon it in favor of mental education? but rather, What form of bodily training and practice is appropriate to the age of the learner? As we shall see, Whitehead's philosophy of education is pervaded with this question of the appropriateness of the phases of education to one another and to the developing self. Much of the physical and some of the mental development of the human being comes about automatically, but the all-important cultural and educational factors require human guidance. For better or worse, this is the task that education faces: to complete what merely biological evolution has begun. An interesting question now arises: Should the educational process strive for the same sort of retracing of steps by which the race has become human? Should the educational rule as well as the strictly biological one be "Ontogeny recapitulates phylogeny"?

As we have seen elsewhere in the present volume, Dewey faces the same question in his own way. What about Whitehead; was he aware of this rule of ontogeny as an educational doctrine? The answer is that Whitehead quite explicitly recognizes this rule at one point, and in a context which immediately leads to the central features of his educational theory.

The preceding account has been necessarily an interpretation. The physical theory (relativity), the biological theory (evolu-

[7] *The Aims of Education and Other Essays* (New York, Macmillan, and London, Ernest Benn, Ltd., 1929, and New American Library of World Literature, 1949), p. 78 [60].

tion), and the metaphysical theory (the inseparability of the physical and mental aspects of reality) are all explicitly and frequently referred to in Whitehead's philosophical writings. The three doctrines are of central importance to the analysis of the human self.[8] Physically, the human person is a complex family of continuous processes; biologically, he is an evolved organism embodying a history of millions of years; metaphysically, he is a creature of inseparable mentality and physicality. But to be is to be an individual. Thus the three theories are ways of narrowing our approach to the individual. To view the individual as a whole we must use the theories together.

We must now consider the specific features of the educational theory, showing how they reflect the more general theories and how they lead on to rather concrete educational proposals. We begin with the explicit reference to evolution as a model.

IV

THE FUNCTIONS OF THE TEACHER

. . . The principle of progress is from within: the discovery is made by ourselves, the discipline is self-discipline, and the fruition is the outcome of our initiative. The teacher has a double function. It is for him to elicit the enthusiasm by resonance from his own personality, and to create the environment of a larger knowledge and a firmer purpose. He is there to avoid the waste, which in the lower stages of existence is nature's way of evolution.[9]

The passage is rich in meaning. The teacher must overcome the insufficiency which characterizes a subhuman evolution. Evolution continues, but for better or worse much of human evolution is under human control itself. The more primitive

[8] Nathaniel Lawrence, "Nature and the Educable Self in Whitehead," *Philosophical Essays: Louisiana State University Studies in Philosophy* (to be published by Louisiana State University Press), has a more detailed account of this analysis.
[9] *Aims of Education*, p. 62 [51].

stages of evolution are groping, unconscious, experimental. New possibilities for evolution are concentrated in the mental capacities of men and must be attended to, by conscious guidance.

The teacher has a double role: (1) In him are concentrated the resources of the race — what it has to offer to the essential capacity of the human animal for becoming a human being, and (2) he must call forth the all-powerful factor of motivation from within the student. But this calling forth is not a matter of creating motivation, implanting it, or even stirring it up. It is a question of focusing and guiding what is already present. "Education," says Whitehead, "must essentially be a *setting in order* of a ferment already stirring in the mind. . . ."[10] Such a ferment is characterized by an innate "passion for discovery,"[11] and this is more than Aristotle's desire to know. Aristotle saw human nature and the laws of science as unchanging, eternally the same. The desire to know was the natural impulse of the child to take his rightful place in the order of things. From Whitehead we get a different picture, a sense that there is a natural creative pressure in life itself underlying the creative development of more intricate and powerful life systems from simpler ones — and surging up anew in each human being, who now stands on the growing edge of mankind evolving. However, we all know the teacher of whom it is said, "He's stimulating, but . . ." or "She's an exciting teacher; however. . . ." There must be also the setting in order, the discipline.

We also know the teacher of whom it is said: "a disciplinarian," and nothing more. Discipline, however, has a natural source; the subject matter should be not only exciting but demanding.[12] Discipline arises from the job to be done, basically. The teacher's discipline is unsuccessful unless the discipline is required by the need for development, the passion for discovery; "the only discipline, important for its own sake, is self-discipline. . . ."[13]

Here we have the threefold function of the teacher:
1. Into his hands has fallen a nearly dread task — to further

10 *Ibid.*, p. 29 [30]; italics ours.   11 *Ibid.*, p. 74 [57].
12 *Ibid.*, pp. 54–57 [45–47] and *passim*.   13 *Ibid.*, p. 55 [46].

the evolution of his race by a constant combing out of the false
starts in human learning and understanding, saving that which
is alive, still productive, and likely to be more than merely
reproductive. Whitehead reinforces the theme:

> Knowledge is the reminiscence by the individual of the
> experience of the race. But reminiscence is never simple re-
> production. The present reacts upon the past. It selects, it
> emphasizes, it adds. The additions are the new ideas by means
> of which the life of the present reflects itself upon the past.[14]

The teacher's task is that of conserving the worthwhile elements and compacting them so that what was before the
whole of human achievement is now compressed to the worthy
parts alone, leaving the way open for an advance which can
never be achieved by society massively, but only by its finest
minds, unhampered by past errors. To the familiar quarrel
between conservatism and progressivism in education the answer is perfectly clear: the quarrel is spurious.

> There are two principles inherent in the very nature of
> things, recurring in some particular embodiments whatever
> field we explore — the spirit of change, and the spirit of
> conservation. There can be nothing real without both. Mere
> change without conservation is a passage from nothing to
> nothing. Its final integration yields mere transient non-entity.
> Mere conservation without change cannot conserve.[15]

Progressive activities depend on the solid foundation of con-
served values. Conversely, a conservation which holds fast to
all that has been will end by conserving little or nothing. The
pressure for reform will build up to a revolutionary threshold
and overflow it, if there is no evolution. Consider the orgy of
progressive education in the early part of the century, much
of it falsely attributed to Dewey. Progressive education over-
flowed the banks of the conservative tradition, washing away
levees that have hardly yet been restored. For education to

---

[14] *Essays in Science and Philosophy* (New York, Philosophical Library,
1947, reprinted in paperback, n.d.), p. 202 [212].
[15] *Science and the Modern World*, p. 289 [201].

progress, there must be both a constant hold on those over-arching concepts which change very slowly and a constant willingness to bring them under review.

> The art of reasoning consists in getting hold of the subject at the right end, of seizing on the few general ideas which illuminate the whole, and of persistently marshalling all subsidiary facts round them. Nobody can be a good reasoner unless by constant practice he has realised the importance of getting hold of the big ideas and of hanging on to them like grim death.[16]

Again, "Do not teach too many subjects. . . . What you teach, teach thoroughly."[17] The practical need is transparent; we can see through it to the doctrine of progress. "We must remember that the whole problem of intellectual education is controlled by lack of time."[18]

The primary question — and there is nothing easy about it — is what to jettison, what to modify, and what to preserve. To assume the posture of progressive or conservative, per se, is as dull-witted in education as it is in politics. Secondly, it is important to notice that the argument as to what to save and what to subordinate is always fraught with practical considerations. No one can provide a guidebook for Saving Only What Is Good. There are always risks and failures. Education must always be prepared to have a growing edge which, like that of nature herself, is sometimes unsuccessful.

2. The second function of the teacher lies not in his powers of discrimination or control but in his personal qualifications. He is a liaison between the individual and society. He brings into personal focus the impersonal collective achievements of his race. This focus is obviously not just a collection of facts. It means an acquaintance with facts as ordered, structured, exhibiting principle, relations, and relations of relations. The creative urge of a developing mind exhibits little in the way of order. It has power but wants organization. "There must be a setting in order of a ferment," Whitehead says. To do this the

---

[16] *Aims of Education*, p. 128 [90–91].
[17] *Ibid.*, p. 2 [14].   [18] *Ibid.*, p. 96 [70].

teacher must devote himself to his subject, so that he has something to teach, to be excited and exciting about.

The last half-century in the United States has seen an almost unchecked spread of courses in teaching methods, teaching psychology, administration, teaching problems, and so on. The overabundance of such courses was the exaggerated result of a needed reform. Before this reform the teacher was at most a kindly warden over innocent prisoners whose ignorance was — hopefully — remediable. With the reform came a flood of nonacademic courses which would be comic if it were not nearly disastrous. The student has changed from a developing organism, rich in possibility and drive, wanting in order and discipline, to a kind of biped guinea pig which should be conditioned, curried, groomed, observed, and well dieted. Or worse, he appears as a part of the great mass of students whom the administrator must regard as a source of problems, stresses, and strains of all sorts. How often is it realized that successful teaching to interested students might well undermine many administrative problems at their sources? The case of problems arising from morale is obvious. Probably no part of American education is in worse condition than this one of teacher preparation. It is not uncommon for a teacher to complain of having spent more time studying how to teach his subject than he has in studying the subject. And we have all known high school students who discovered to their dismay that their competence exceeded that of their teachers.

Since the student is a living organism, a complex processive pattern, there is always the "problem of keeping knowledge alive."[19] Motivation, drive, attention — these will always be present. The great question is, "What will guide or attract them?" "Knowledge," says Whitehead, "is a process, adding content and control to the flux of experience."[20] The student is alive, and the knowledge is supposed to be integral to him and his life. Whitehead means what he says, literally. The human mind is neither a tool nor in any sense a container. "The pupil's mind is a growing organism. On the one hand, it is not a box to be ruthlessly packed with alien ideas: and,

[19] *Ibid.*, p. 7 [17].
[20] *Essays in Science and Philosophy*, p. 214 [225].

on the other hand, the ordered acquirement of knowledge is the natural food for a developing intelligence."[21] Again: ". . . education is not a process of packing articles in a trunk . . . Its nearest analogue is the assimilation of food by a living organism."[22] "The mind is never passive; it is a perpetual activity, delicate, receptive, responsive to stimulus. You cannot postpone its life until you have sharpened it."[23] "The pupils have got to be made to feel that they are studying something, and are not merely executing intellectual minuets."[24]

The terms "food," "nourishment," and "organism" are instructive. Teachers trained largely in methods instead of in their subjects may very well be in the position of cooks with much silverware and little food.

3. Finally, the teacher appears as the *exposer* of discipline. What is important here is to get rid of the idea of discipline as something added to subject matter. Either the discipline arises from the nature of the subject matter or its worth is in doubt. It is the teacher's task to bring out the interest and the demand of the subject matter as two aspects of the same thing.

Discipline underlies the possibility of future self-education. The student is an organism which not only develops but learns to develop. We can guide the development while he is our student, but what of the development that he must undertake *for himself* when he is no longer under our tutelage? We forget, says Whitehead, "that we are only subordinate elements in the education of a grown man; and that, in their own good time, in later life our pupils will learn for themselves."[25]

Will they? That is the teacher's nightmare. We are close here to the basic dilemma of the teaching profession. In no profession is the result of one's effort so far out of sight; in no secular profession is faith so strongly needed. Rarely does a teacher follow a student's progress, much less contribute to it, for more than four years. Then what? Once in a while a student comes back; once in a long while one can see the fruit of his labor. With the real results lying over the horizon, the teacher all too often tries to assure himself of his worth by

[21] *Aims of Education*, p. 47 [41].
[22] *Ibid.*, p. 51 [44].
[23] *Ibid.*, p. 9 [18].
[24] *Ibid.*, p. 15 [21].
[25] *Ibid.*, p. 53 [45].

imposing a heavy load of *external* discipline. Tests, reports, and summary grades — undoubtedly these serve to indicate a student's progress and measure the quality of his achievement. They are also balms to the teacher, whose chronic frustration in working for an end he never sees leads him to seek reassurance that something has been accomplished right now. But, "There can be no mental development without interest. ... You may endeavour to excite interest by means of birch rods, or you may coax it by the incitement of pleasurable activity. But without interest there will be no progress."[26] You cannot merely teach your subject, you must lead the student in such a way that there will be an internal drive toward self-development when the external structures of formal education are taken off. "Cursed be the dullard," says Whitehead, "who destroys wonder."[27]

Whitehead insists that the students as well as the teachers learn the lesson of self-motivation toward self-development. In an unusual speech to a group of technical school boys he presses the theme of their individual responsibility.

> You cannot begin to understand nature's method unless you grasp the fact that the essential spring of all growth is within you. All that you can get from without is some food, material or spiritual, with which to build your own organism, and some stimulus to spur you to activity. What is really essential in your development you must do for yourselves. The regular method of nature is a happy process of genial encouragement. There can be very little satisfactory growth with the exclusion of this method.[28]

Moreover, the inducing of such motivation cannot be carried on without pleasure. Joy and pleasure have their role:

> Joy is the normal healthy spur for the *élan vital*. I am not maintaining that we can safely abandon ourselves to the allurement of the greater immediate joys. What I do mean is that we should seek to arrange the development of character along a path of natural activity, in itself pleasurable. The

26 *Ibid.*, p. 48 [42].   27 *Ibid.*, pp. 50–51 [43].
28 *Essays in Science and Philosophy*, p. 171 [179].

subordinate stiffening of discipline must be directed to secure some long-time good; although an adequate object must not be too far below the horizon, if the necessary interest is to be retained.[29]

The lesson is simple to repeat, hard to follow: If imposed discipline is not ultimately espoused by the student for himself, it will not last beyond the teacher's presence, but the espousal must arise basically from application or use.

In the process of learning there should be present, in some sense or other, a subordinate activity of application. In fact, the applications are part of the knowledge. For the very meaning of the things known is wrapped up in their relationships beyond themselves. Thus unapplied knowledge is knowledge shorn of its meaning.[30]

Needless to say, not all use must be tangible or "practical," but for discipline to be welcomed and taken in, its worth must be known. "The only discipline, important for its own sake, is self-discipline."

The implications of this doctrine of discipline are hardly escapable. There are three phases of human development: (1) the physical development, which is largely automatic, within broad limits of suitable nourishment and environment; (2) the dependent mental development, which is largely nonautomatic (mental development requires skilled selection of subject matter — "suitable nourishment" — and acute guidance in the rhythmic phases through which a subject naturally unfolds — "environment"); (3) the independent mental development, which resembles the automatic physical development in not being stimulated primarily from the outside but is like the dependent development in that it occurs under conscious guidance — in this case one's own guidance. Phase (1) is man as a physical animal. Phase (2) is man as a thinking being. Phase (3) is man as a person, which is to say a thinking being, self-disciplined. The grounding of Whitehead's philosophy in the

[29] *Aims of Education*, p. 49 [42].
[30] *Essays in Science and Philosophy*, p. 219 [230].

doctrine of evolution is obvious; the three phases described are the major phases in the evolution of a human individual.

We have come by way of a survey of what is involved in the modern view of the world to a rough analysis of human nature, showing what human nature requires in the function of the teacher. We are thus led to the curricular process in which student and teacher are engaged.

V

The Curricular Process

Education is a continuous process of growth. From within the student himself arises a raw urge toward development, but beyond a certain primitive level there is no self-regulating direction or organization. The ever widening society of the developing child supplies some help, but the packed formative years from two to twenty require skilled professional guidance if the student is to realize his latent abilities. These years cover the period of formal education for most students. What principles underlie the formation and use of the curriculum? A curriculum is literally, in Latin, a running, a racecourse. How should the course be laid out?

There is a natural rhythm, says Whitehead, that flows through all educational development. It has three main phases. In the phase of enthusiastic encounter whatever is at hand is interesting, attractive for itself, though bad teaching may kill the interest before any progress is made in the subject. Arithmetic is a common example. Whitehead calls this first stage the *Romantic* stage. The second stage, in which order and system are introduced, is the period in which the chronology of history (rather than just its tales), the grammar of language, and so on, should appear. Whitehead calls this the stage of *Precision*. The final phase, which, properly handled, is the beginning of a new romantic phase, is the one in which precision has done its work. In this phase the student, with an understanding of both the surface aspects and the structure of his study, is prepared to extend his knowledge in the direction of acquiring and putting into order more of the world about him. In understanding an order he has a systematic view in which to place what he finds, and from which he can advance. This stage Whitehead calls the stage of *Generalization*.

We shall return shortly to an elaboration of these stages, but now a question arises. How does Whitehead know that this pattern is the right one, and why should we see it so? The answer is that the educational process is but one type of growth process and it conforms to a natural pattern to be found in *any* process where something genuinely comes into being rather than merely repeating itself, as in the motion of a machine, whose processes are not organic. This pattern Whitehead calls a rhythm. In a noneducational work he warns us that we are to look for rhythms throughout nature, even in the most simplified kind of existence. Expositors of his views on education have largely ignored this revolutionary conception: that the patterns of education are continuous with and basically like those of the whole of nature. "The Way of Rhythm," says Whitehead, "pervades all life, and indeed all physical existence. The common principle of Rhythm is one of the reasons for believing that *the root principles of life are, in some lowly form, exemplified in all types of physical existence.*"[31]

We are twice required to take a brief look at these "lowly forms" present in "physical existence." First, the human being himself is a complex of physical processes. Some of these processes operate largely automatically, but others we expect to come under the guidance of education. Second, these "lowly" forms of rhythm will give us a simple model of the more complex growth processes which constitute our lives.

What makes up processes? Events, occurrences, happenings. The process of electing a President, for instance, begins with the millions of single events which are the castings of votes. These are drawn together in groups, and these groups into still others, until through the electoral college a President is chosen. The election is a single, complex event made up of subordinate ones. One usually analyzes a process into its events, the events

[31] *Function of Reason*, pp. 16–17 [21]; italics ours.

being finally reduced to the things or objects which behave some way in space and time. The rock moved through space for a certain period of time; its speed and its weight combined, on contact, to break the window. But the new physics tells us there is no separate space and time, in which some material stuff resides and behaves. These ideas are only practical conveniences in ordinary affairs. The rock itself, on closer analysis, is a swarm of fields of electromagnetic activity, i.e., processes composed of events. The formula is simple: Events are composed of other events, down to the simplest single event that there can be, a unit event which occurs in a minimum extent of time. The least event that can occur and still be an event Whitehead calls "an actual occasion."[32]

An actual occasion is a single pulse of being, but it has discernible parts. There are three main phases of its coming into existence. (1) Conceived as having no reference to anything else, an actual occasion is simply a burst of creative novelty. In a human being the creative novelty is the origin of what Whitehead calls the "ferment," or "passion," which must be both guided and nourished. But, of course, there is no such thing as an entity which has *no* reference at all to anything else. For instance, it shares a common spatiality with other actual things. The actual occasion is a burst of creativity, but it arises from a background of past fact. It is from this realm of past fact that the actual occasion literally makes itself, taking account of the antecedent world. (2) The taking account of the diverse data of the past is not a mere absorption. It is a harmonizing, a placing together of the elements of the past, those repeatable elements which Whiteheads calls "eternal objects," in various ways that will make them combinable into a single entity, the actual occasion. (3) The third phase is that of completion; Whitehead says of it that it "closes up the entity." This is the stage in which the actual occasion, by becoming internally complete, ceases and becomes "objectively immortal." Nothing more of a creative sort happens "inside"

[32] *Process and Reality*, p. 113. The more technical features of this entity are discussed in Lawrence, "Nature and the Educable Self in Whitehead," *op. cit.*

it. It is over and done with, but it remains as something for future actual occasions to take account of in one way or another, in their own self-composition.

The term "actual occasion" designates the unit organism, the least building block of reality. The term may refer to a single pulse of existence in the life of an electron; in this case it will have taken account of the antecedent world only in a very limited way, for one segment in the vibratory existence of an electron is much like the last and the next. But the term "actual occasion" may equally refer to an instant of consciousness in a human life, gathering together swarms of antecedent memories, perceptions, feelings, and so forth, so as to display the greatest originality and novelty. Education should fund and harmoniously order the events which are gathered into the continuous development of the person. Such an enriching of his personal resources must give him maximum opportunities for future self-realization. It is only a short step from this educational ideal to the often neglected point that the more specialized an adult occupation a man is to have, the greater the need for a prior breadth in the training of his understanding. If his life is to be one of routine specialization, and only that, then it is worth less than the automated device that can be programmed to replace him.

The significance of the actual occasion is that although its life span is by definition as brief as possible, it is nevertheless a true organism. It therefore exhibits, in simplest form, all the phases of existence which characterize the existence of any organism, simple or complex, either long lasting or quickly perishing. The human organism is an incredibly complicated network of subordinate organisms which serve and support him; and his educational development must be understood and directed in terms of the repeated cycles of his growth. But the basic model for these cycles is the minute actual occasion. In a similar way biological life processes are often studied in their simplest form in the cell, of which more complex organisms are composed.

Let us see how these three rhythmic phases of an organism appear in the educational process.

1. *Romance*

Just as the first phase of the actual occasion is one of a sheer ingathering, so is the first phase in the educative development of a human being. In this phase, says Whitehead, "knowledge is not dominated by systematic procedure."[33] This is the stage of the "ferment" referred to earlier, when "The subject-matter has the vividness of novelty; it holds within itself unexplored connexions with possibilities half-disclosed by glimpses and half-concealed by the wealth of material."[34] The Romantic phase cyclically recurs with deeper and deeper penetration of the surrounding world. With the preschool child it takes the form of "apprehension of objects" and "coordination of its perceptions with its bodily activities."[35] Later comes the Romantic encounter with literature, art, history, in which discipline and system are of less importance than the inciting of the youth to "kindred activities."[36] Finally comes the Romantic encounter with science, in early adolescence. "The pupils should see for themselves, and experiment for themselves, with only fragmentary precision of thought."[37]

The stage of Romance is a familiar one. It is the stage of excitement, interest, espousal. On this stage much of progressive education rested its starry hopes. Having discovered that immature motivation was important in its own right, progressive education often jettisoned discipline to an appalling degree. A story is told of a British child, increasingly restive before her return to her progressive school. On the last day of vacation she burst into tears and cried, "Mommy, when I go back to school, will I have to do exactly what I want to do?" Isn't there always a passion for order too? The baby wants a stable world with a regularity of its own which he can depend upon. Why should this appetite vanish when he is old enough to go to school? Moreover, growth requires not merely creative expression and assimilation. It must have an orderly continuity and structure which makes further orderly growth possible; otherwise it is merely cancerous.

Here is one point at which the skill and sensitivity of the

---

[33] *Aims of Education*, p. 28 [29].   [34] *Ibid.*
[35] *Ibid.*, p. 31.   [36] *Ibid.*, p. 34 [33].   [37] *Ibid.*, p. 37 [35]

teacher become most important. When does the high school teacher, for example, lead the student from his surface appreciation of T. S. Eliot's poetry into the analysis of the strict technique of Eliot's writing? At what point does he introduce the student to the mathematical method in the analysis of biological studies? Certainly not before the results to be obtained can be vaguely discerned and desired, but also not *merely* with the student's recognition that something is wanting in his own understanding. The student must be acquainted with the nature of his ignorance before he can get rid of it. The stage of Precision opens gradually out of that of Romance, but the emergence of the second stage must have its reasonableness in the subject matter. Otherwise the discipline is arbitrary and ineffective.

2. *Precision*

The second phase in the rhythm of education is that of Precision. It corresponds exactly to the phase in the actual occasion in which the entity organizes, harmonizes, and orders the diverse data it has acquired from the antecedent world. This phase, of course, "is barren without a previous stage of romance. . . ."[38] "New facts are added, but they are the facts which fit into the analysis."[39] It is the period of grammar in language,[40] principles and laws in science and mathematics,[41] and memorizing in history.[42]

The stage of Precision is thus what was commonly regarded before progressivism as the whole of education. Get things right, get them thoroughly, and get them in order. Adulthood will be with you soon. Prepare yourself for the mantle of maturity! Now Whitehead's point is that the demands of Precision are inescapable, but they have a restricted place in the rhythm of education. They come *after* the romantic encounter and are justified by that encounter. Why bother with grammar; why not let the forms of the language rub off on the student through repeated exposure? Because he will have need of a strop on which to sharpen his own capacities for

---

[38] *Ibid.*, p. 29 [30].   [39] *Ibid.*   [40] *Ibid.*
[41] *Ibid.*, p. 38 [35].   [42] *Ibid.*, p. 35 [33].

expression. The grammar of a language is its living logic. The student will want to know, and know instinctively, through habitual analysis of the structure of a sentence, whether what he hears and reads is rhetorically persuasive alone or logically sound. There is an interesting correlation between the decline of the teaching of structural grammar and the collapse of letter writing, on the one hand, and, on the other, the rise in gullibility to the use of mass media for political and advertising purposes. Yet literacy is supposed to be increasing. What then is the test of literacy? The number of people going to school or the results of their going to school?

There is a final point to be made about the need for early doses of discipline. This is the phase in which the student's strong points will emerge, tested by exacting demands.[43] At that point in his education when he is thinking of his future profession, he needs to know more than what he is "interested" or even "talented" in. He needs to know in what kind of work he is willing to do hard, exacting, and detailed study. Colleges are plagued with high-testing students who believe that professions are chosen on the basis of interest and expect the teachers to supply the interest. Only a self-disciplined mind can rise to a higher level of understanding, where a new Romantic cycle begins.

3. *Generalization*

Whitehead says of the third and final stage of the actual occasion that it is that of satisfaction. Of the final stage of the educational cycle he says it is "Hegel's synthesis. It is a return to romanticism with added advantage of classified ideas and relevant technique. It is the fruition which has been the goal of the precise training. It is the final success."[44] This stage is clearly a "reaction toward romance."[45] In this sense, "The stage of precision is the stage of growing into the apprehension of principles by the acquisition of a precise knowledge of details. The stage of generalisations is the stage of shedding details in favour of the active application of principles, the

43 *Ibid.*, pp. 39–40 [36–37].
44 *Ibid.*, p. 30 [30–31].　　　　　45 *Ibid.*, p. 57 [47].

details retreating into subconscious habits."[46] Thus with the appearance of Generalization the cycle starts over.

The romance inherent in Generalization is that of research and writing. All true research and much creativity must begin with Generalization. A *re*-search presupposes an initial search. Mushrooms develop suddenly, "overnight," as everyone knows. But who knows how or why? No one knew twenty years ago. Yet the experiments that showed why were within the technical grasp of biologists a hundred years ago. The Bible contradicts itself, yet it embodies truths which we can hardly wave away. What shall we do, jettison scripture and start over again or swallow it whole? If we discriminate, then on what basis and why? The barefoot genius in art or literature soon loses his force. If he has no acquaintance with the field in which he creates, he has but little critical acumen as to what he should modify, what adapt, and what leave behind as mined out. The capacity to generalize plus some luck and curiosity are the basis for genuine advance in human understanding. In it lies the possibility of progress.

What is true of the educational cycle in particular is true of all organic cycles in general. The passage quoted early in this section from the *Function of Reason* continues with this remark: "In the Way of Rhythm . . . the end of one such cycle is the proper antecedent stage for the beginning of another such cycle."[47] Romance must be followed by Precision. Precision sets the stage for the ascent to a higher level, that of Generalization. And from the higher ground new vistas appear. A new stage of Romance is begun.

In conclusion, the clear picture of these phases must be qualified in three ways. (1) There are no sharp lines of division between the phases. One grades into another, ideally without jars or breaks, the phases of the cycle being a matter of emphasis at any given time.[48] (2) There are cycles overlapping cycles. Language may be in a precise stage when the romance of science has just begun; in fact, perhaps it should be, for the mere recording of interesting scientific facts relies upon the

[46] *Ibid.*, p. 58 [48].
[47] *Function of Reason*, p. 17 [21].
[48] *Aims of Education*, p. 44 [40].

capacity to use language with precision. (3) There are cycles within cycles. Even the individual lesson "should form an eddy cycle issuing in its own subordinate process."[49] From the overlap of cycles of education and the inclusion of smaller cycles in larger ones arises the rhythmic continuity of the educational process, through which an individual continuously exists, yet changes and grows.

VI

THE AIM OF EDUCATION

The aim of education is to help in the self-production of a person, to secure for him a "balanced growth of individuality."[50] The self-production arises from an innate "passion" which must be fed and satisfied from the collective resources of the society. As the person develops, the processes which make up his life become more various and more intricate. At one stage the baby digests only milk. At one stage the young child's greatest verbal development lies in the use of simple nouns and adjectives. Development means the appearance of new capacities and new skills, somehow integrated with the old. Throughout there is a continuous identity. This process is something like converting a rowboat to an ocean liner while the boat is in continuous service. The sound keel of past experience must be capitalized upon and lengthened. This is the source of "precision." Present need and present enthusiasm supply the motivation for the increased accommodation of new understanding. This is the source of "romanticism." But without generalization there is no stable deck on which to build future accommodations. Creative self-development rests upon it. This is one reason for the breadth of education at the college level. In an age of specialization no one advances in a profitable way whose general perspective is confined to his own specialty.

---

[49] *Ibid.*, p. 30 [31]. It is the term "process" which in cosmology comes to be the fundamental term in all description of actuality.
[50] *Science and the Modern World*, p. 284 [197].

The "balanced growth" which education aims to secure is constantly threatened. Curiously, it is threatened by progress itself. Whitehead once remarked that virtually every scientific conception which he learned in his youth had been either swept away or sharply modified. The rate of progress, he says, "is such that an individual human being, of ordinary length of life, will be called upon to face novel situations which find no parallel in his past."[51] The result is that the "fixed person for the fixed duties," formerly a godsend, in the future will be a "public danger." Yet knowledge that is effective is "professionalised knowledge, supported by a restricted acquaintance with useful subjects subservient to it."[52]

The common way of attempting to avoid the dilemma is to aim at an education which provides both the special professional training and general knowledge. But Whitehead is dubious about balancing a deep study of a few abstractions with a shallow study of many abstractions. "The make-weight which balances the thoroughness of the specialist intellectual training should be of a radically different *kind* from purely intellectual analytical knowledge."[53] If the ailment of education lies in its abstractness, the breadth of a group of abstractions only spuriously balances the depth of another group.

What is this different kind of experience which must be present in education?

What I mean is art and aesthetic education. It is, however, art in such a general sense of the term that I hardly like to call it by that name. Art is a special example. What we want is to draw out habits of aesthetic apprehension. . . . Thus "art" in the general sense which I require is any selection by which the concrete facts are so arranged as to elicit attention to particular values which are realisable by them.[54]

Art, so conceived, may refer equally to sunsets or factories. If we undertake merely to treat the sunset in terms of the atmosphere, rotation of the earth, and so on, or the factory as a

[51] *Ibid.*, p. 282 [196].   [52] *Ibid.*
[53] *Ibid.*, p. 285 [198]; italics ours.
[54] *Ibid.*, pp. 286–287 [199–200].

device for making salable products, we are engaged in the kind of abstraction which robs the soul of its need for value. We slip into such abstractions all the more readily if the educational pattern is forever training us to deal with abstractions alone. "This fertilisation of the soul is the reason for the necessity of art. . . . The soul cries aloud for release into change. . . . [But] great art is more than a transient refreshment. It is something which adds to the permanent richness of the soul's self-attainment."[55]

These reflections of Whitehead come in mid-passage in his philosophical career, years after the major part of his educational writings. They constitute an important reflection on those writings. He has before him the major features of his own educational theory, but these features are now seen in a different perspective. The level of Generalization has a new significance. It is not merely a return to Romance in that it provides us new vistas with fresh encounters looming. It is also a return to Romance in that it must include concrete confrontation with value. Precision is content with assuming the values of the things which it orders. Having devoted myself to the value of designing commercial buildings, I may, in the phase of Precision, acquire all the engineering and technical knowledge of materials required to practice my profession. But these buildings are sociological and aesthetic structures as well. The danger of professional precision is that it will never rise to the level of generalization where it is related to the values it will effect. "The type of generality," says Whitehead, "which above all is wanted, is the appreciation of the variety of value. I mean an aesthetic growth."[56] Professional training, which "can only touch one side of education," largely depending on printed books, must be balanced by concrete contact with things perceived as being values for one another.[57]

This is Whitehead's final word on the aim of education. He presents us with the picture of an actually physical, potentially mental organism, whose orderly growth depends on the skill with which the various cycles are interknit and inclusive of one another. Ideally they achieve upward and outward spirals

[55] *Ibid.*, pp. 290–291 [202].
[56] *Ibid.*, p. 286 [199].   [57] *Ibid.*

of progress. But not only must they never be divorced from their use; they must also strive toward a generalization which can only be acquired by an aesthetic return to the concrete particulars that make up the context of each life.

Contemporary education faces a unique problem: a violent expansion in factual knowledge, analogous to the population explosion. But facts in isolation are by definition valueless. It is in the relation of facts to one another and to men that their value lies. Our romantic encounter with facts soon requires a precise rendering of them in an orderly and disciplined way. Thus we are poised on the edge of generality. The power to generalize requires the ability to abstract. But a preoccupation with abstraction disconnects us from reality. True generalization needs constantly to be balanced by a continuous contact with those actual aspects of the world which one's own restricted pursuits influence and effect. The time for developing this habit of perspective is during formal education. Otherwise, education collapses at the point that adulthood appears. Generalization, Whitehead would say, is for the sake of education, not vice versa.

Beyond a presentation of the place of conventional studies in English schools, we get no precise curricular recommendation from Whitehead. Who can foretell for all time what demands will be made on education? But he does give us an invariant pattern of *method* in the three phases through which any educational unit, great or small, must pass, and a conception of the achievement of the method, which is a generality of *personal* outlook, rather than the intellectual control of abstract generalization.

Suggestions for Further Reading

Whitehead's explicit views on education are found not only in *The Aims of Education* (New York, Macmillan, 1929, and Mentor Books, 1949) but at a later stage in the concluding chapter ("Requisites for Social Progress") of his *Science and the Modern World* (New York, Macmillan, 1925, and Mentor Books, 1948). The *Introduction to Mathematics* (New York, Holt, 1929), now available in paperback (Galaxy Books, 1959), invites comparison with the current work of the School Mathematics Study Group. Concentrating on the "main ideas" and treating in succession number, position, shape, functions, series, geometry, and quantity, it presents a twentieth-century version of what the Middle Ages were trying to do in the Quadrivium. The asides and concrete examples, together with the love of formal clarity and rigor, both illustrate the theories of *The Aims of Education*.

Most of Whitehead's writings can be read without too much difficulty; they are on the whole nontechnical, excellently written, and excitingly original. These include *Religion in the Making* (New York, Macmillan, 1926, and Living Age Books, 1960), where the contrast between his and Dewey's views of the "self" comes out most clearly; *Adventures of Ideas* (New York, Macmillan, 1933, and Mentor Books, 1955); *Modes of Thought* (New York, Macmillan, 1938, and Capricorn Books, 1959,), *Symbolism* (New York, Macmillan, 1927, and Capricorn Books, 1959); and *The Function of Reason* (Princeton, Princeton University Press, 1929, and Boston, Beacon, 1958).

Process and Reality (New York, Macmillan, 1929, and Harper Torchbooks, 1960), on the other hand, is difficult in the extreme. It is Whitehead's principal technical work in philosophy. In it he revises and enlarges some of his earlier views. Only students with considerable study in philosophy should undertake this volume.

There are now some helpful studies of Whitehead available. Among them are Nathaniel Lawrence, *Whitehead's Philosophical Development* (Berkeley, University of California Press, 1956); W. A. Christian, *An Interpretation of Whitehead's Metaphysics* (New Haven, Yale University Press, 1959); Donald Sherburne, *A Whiteheadian Aesthetic* (New Haven, Yale University Press, 1961); and, in another dimension of Whitehead's thought, R. M. Palter, *Whitehead's Philosophy of Science* (Chicago, University of Chicago Press, 1960). Ivor LeClerc, *Whitehead's Metaphysics: an Introductory Exposition* (New York, Macmillan, 1958), is a primer for students with some philosophical background and is written in a straightforward way; it covers the principal features of a vast and complicated terrain. Victor Lowe's *Understanding Whitehead* (Baltimore, Johns Hopkins Press, 1962), which is somewhat longer, can be begun by someone with philosophical interest but no particular philosophical training. As it progresses, it more and more presumes a wide interest in philosophy, from the philosophy of religion to the philosophy of physical science.

CHAPTER EIGHT

Conclusion

I

SOME CONTEMPORARY PROBLEMS

The abiding value of Plato's educational philosophy is widely diffused in contemporary education. Plato's thought takes many forms because of much useful modification. But one notion comes to us relatively unaltered: There are many aspects to reality; accordingly, there are many aspects to education. The various aspects of education rely upon one another, however, and any effort to make one aspect dominant and independent of the rest is (unwittingly) aimed at shaping minds with a distorted sense of reality. The sense of reality and the aims of education at any given time interact and are interdependent. In the Middle Ages the dominant intellectual doctrine about reality was that it lay beyond our brief earthly existence. The latter was simply a moral proving ground, a kind of antechamber to heaven or hell. The earth is the Lord's and they that dwell therein. His will is done on earth, and His ways are unsearchable. The medieval sense of reality did little to encourage men to seek sanitation, health, or intellectual cultivation. As long as the uncritical acceptance of authority, disease, pestilence, famine, and war could be given a religious explanation, the sense of the unreality of this world and men's failure to better their condition reinforced each other.

We are in an opposite position now, one of extreme individualistic materialism. Individual opinion is courted by politicians, advertisers, and pollsters. And the values admired, sought, and exchanged, fought for to the literal death, are largely materialistic; comfort, possessions, power, photographable beauty underlie a sickeningly large number of our allegedly diverse aims. History will show the mid-twentieth century as being as unbalanced as the time of the Inquisition.

If education is lopsided, the prevailing sense of reality will be distorted. If the public sense of real value is lopsided, the educational pattern will become further lopsided. If we are to keep to Plato's ideal of the interlocking aspects of education, the educational system itself must be relatively independent of fluctuation in public opinion. Ideally, education should lead the public, not vice versa. But to do this it must be self-critical, and constantly so. Teachers need to be experts in their subjects, and more far-seeing than the parents of their students. If they are amateurs, or if they fall into myopic routines, they cannot complain if the school board proposes to guide their activities. The real expert is in a position to quiet the interfering layman by getting better results than the layman could.

We are indebted to Plato for the idea of an expert educator whose tangible worth lies in the results he gets. We also receive from him the idea of a multifaceted reality which is the object of a multifaceted educational search. But the idea of an evolving social order and an evolving human nature, requiring continuous self-criticism, is a contemporary one. For these conceptions we turn to men like Dewey and Whitehead.

The conception of the educator as an expert is a tenacious Platonic notion. It is not dispensable. It is essential to the idea of civilization as cumulative in its achievements. It also bears on one of the most pressing contemporary problems, namely, teachers' salaries. Over the last three decades the economic place of the teacher has steadily gone down. Yet never has the public expectation of his profession run so high. The teaching profession could conceivably suffer the downward spiral that has occurred in the ministry, where a combination of poor training and low salaries has assisted in the decline of a leading profession. Nowadays the young college instructor gets a part-time job as a teller in the bank. The high school history teacher "moonlights" as a part-time carpenter. Their institutions pay them part-time salaries and get part-time services in return. It is not hard to hear a striking Canadian doctor, who refuses to practice under his government's legalization of socialized medicine, say, "What! Work for the government? Look what happens to teachers who do!" There are more teaching jobs than there are selfless public spirits and martyrs. If America wants expert education, she must pay for it, and if she doesn't want expert education, she must be prepared to step aside and let other nations go ahead.[1] The problem of teachers' salaries is but one case of a practical problem that quickly taps back to a philosophical issue. The idea of the teacher as expert raises the question of his central role in society, his public function, and his relation to the human soul. These questions cannot be solved piecemeal or *ad hoc*.

Coordinate with the teacher's relatively low salary is the relatively high cost of the physical plant, its facilities, and its overhead. Aside from the familiar but shameful economic subordination of the libraries to restaurants, stadiums, and sports pavilions, another question has arisen: Shall we pour money into teaching machines, televised instruction, and programmed learning, or pay our personnel more appropriate salaries? The question is already of some age, what with the advent of language-teaching records, tapes, and microfilm. Some discussion has taken place, but installation and espousal has outrun it. We are bungling ahead with too little reflection.

Teaching machines have many advantages: low cost, constant access, individually variable learning rates, and so on. The advocates of teaching machines, using the theme implicit in Norbert Wiener's book title, *The Human Use of Human Beings*, point out that machines can take over routines, reducing the teacher shortage and releasing teachers for more imaginative and complex tasks. Well and good. But where do we draw the line between routine and imagination, between those

[1] Fritz Baade, in *The Race to the Year 2000* (New York, Doubleday, 1962), p. 124, quotes the Federal Ministry for Atomic Energy (West Germany) as saying that in Russia the president of a technical institute earns half again as much as the director-in-chief of a major industrial enterprise and that a professor of ten years' standing earns more than a chief engineer.

educational exchanges in which teacher response is all-important and those where it is of no importance? Ask the extreme question for a moment, "Are there any situations in which teacher response is of little or no value?" Kant's warning is essential at this point: he saw more clearly than most thinkers have that a "phenomenal being" can obviously be machine-conditioned to respond as we want him to, automatically, just as a pigeon or a parrot can.[2] B. F. Skinner, a pioneer in the use of teaching machines, says, after a lengthy description of how pigeons can be taught to do such things as pace out a figure eight, that "The power of the technique has to be seen to be believed."[3] He then goes on, "There is a historical connection between Project Pigeon and our teaching machines." Although, he says, the problems are quantitatively more complex, "Why not teach students by machine also?"[4]

Is such conditioning worth much unless the true inner self is engaged as well, making its own decisions, following its own visions? For human beings we will want to keep in view the importance of originality and creativity as aims of education. Do we want to ignore the social values in group learning, which so strongly impressed John Dewey? Both Dewey and Whitehead warn us that our race experience was corporately acquired, not just individually obtained. But Skinner says of his machine that "The effect on each student is surprisingly like that of a private tutor." Do we want the social aspects of education to be excluded? And if we do, are we prepared to imagine the student and the machine taking a conversational trip to the United Nations?

It would be so foolish, at this late date in the history of education, to repeat the mistake of the Sophists in equating knowledge with information, education with a spectator sport of memorizing right answers, that no one is likely to do it deliberately. Through laziness and inadvertence, however, there is a constant temptation to concentrate on things that are technically easy to test and handle. It is obvious that objective tests and information are more easily scored and transmitted

[2] See B. F. Skinner, "Teaching Machines," *Scientific American,* Vol. 205, No. 5 (November, 1961), pp. 90–102.
[3] *Ibid.,* p. 93.   [4] *Ibid.,* p. 95.

than aesthetic insight or ethical creativity. To be experimental, enthusiastic, but above all judicious is the counsel both of common sense and of Western philosophy. Isn't the safest brief thing to say about the present teaching machines that their function ought to be confined to Whitehead's second stage, the stage of "Precision" or "Discipline"? Certainly the impact of these machines will be high. Shall we proceed without reflection, or if with reflection, how deep shall we go into a general philosophy of education to get guidance?

With the introduction of the social aspects of learning comes the most confused and confusing of all the features of contemporary education. It may seem unnecessary and even a bit old-fashioned to insist that practice in social effectiveness is a necessary, and legitimate, part of education. Our schools have been claiming to provide this for the past four decades, and many of their critics believe, with some justification, that they have been overdoing it. Oddities abound, however. Some critics make fun of "social adjustment" taught at the price of discipline, while complaining that high school youth these days are lacking in a sense of social responsibility. The real issue lies to one side of the familiar battlegrounds. The nightmare of intelligent teachers and principals is the unreflective tendency of extremists to assume that the only way anyone can be an effective social being, or a good person at all, is to think as they do. Adaptation is arbitrarily identified with conformity. In the nature of the case, high school students, for instance, cannot think exactly as their parents do; but they can repeat slogans and attitudes, echoing father's damnation of liberals or reactionaries or water fluoridation or the U.N., and this seems to be what many parents define as "thinking." There always used to be one parent of each college senior class who complained to the local administration that his son or daughter was "getting ideas." To which one dean is reported to have said, "Splendid! Can you prove it?" Nowadays, perhaps we all recognize that this is a silly complaint; so instead we say that he or she is "getting the wrong ideas." Wouldn't we do well to cut this out and realize that what is important is not the exact formula our students accept, but whether they have been responsible in examining evidence, and logical in drawing their conclusions from it? Isn't our real aim to see that students become mature and imaginative enough to see the ways in which their notions have practical social consequences? We cannot do our children's thinking for them. Either they do it or else it isn't their thinking. It is destructive of honesty, intelligence, freedom, and society to censor all ideas and materials which are objectionable to some parent or civic group; what a sad pottage of damp platitude is left over, when we do so!

We are not advocating an ideal of paralyzed indecision, sometimes called "seeing both sides of every question." We do not suggest that responsible school officials and teachers give up their practice of selection and run an "anything goes" show with pornography, opium, and subversion welcomed to the classroom. However, high school students will and should encounter some ideas and readings that their parents find objectionable. The role of the teacher is not to keep parents complacent but to see that the material has educational value for the students in his charge. The only way one learns to be a social animal is by being one; the classroom teaches by example, as well as by precept, respect for the rights and opinions of others, democratic ways of making some decisions, responsibility for and to a group of fellow human beings. It is strange to emphasize the teaching of democracy as an abstraction in social studies classes while ignoring the admittedly limited opportunities for practicing it in school and classroom.

One reason "social adjustment" currently has had a bad name in many circles is that it is identified with mediocrity, reliance on group opinion, and timid conformity. Part of the responsibility for this identification lies outside the school where, among other factors, the interlocked economic affairs of society have bred a passion for security and social acceptance that has threatened to annihilate individual self-dependence. Is there, in the nature of things, any reason why social responsibility and courtesy can only be bought at the price of individuality? Much resentment of "society," expressing itself in destructive hostility and beatnikism, is in fact dissatisfaction not with external restrictions but with the failure of that society to develop any awareness that the individual has an intrinsic dignity and an inner self of his own.

The wasteful conflicts of society and individual are not likely to improve much if the claims of each have no concrete place in the educational experience of the citizen to be. Yet how can such experience arise in the educational process if neither student nor teacher asks himself very seriously or persistently what an individual is, what society is, or how they interact and interdepend? The self-propelling, independent man, living close to nature and learning the reasonableness of things by direct contact with the reasons, is a character in a typical Rousseauian romance. The impracticalities of *Émile* tempt us to reject the work as a sentimental fancy. Yet the ideals and their reasonableness must find their way into any philosophy of education which respects individual integrity. Aristotle's ideal, on the other hand, is one of social values transmitted to and through the habituated student, so that the mutually dependent social and rational qualities of the human being can be perfected. Aristotle's perspective is that of the rich city-state, with its inherent possibilities for small-community humaneness and its slave labor for menial tasks. The emphasis on habituated social values could easily result, in the contemporary nationalist state, in a sinister totalitarianism. It is precisely this problem which John Dewey faces when he distinguishes the individual act of thinking from the social treasure of knowledge.

The final immediate practical issue we want to discuss, before we end our brief sketch of applications of philosophy to current concerns, is training in concrete sensitivity. Perhaps if we had not read Whitehead, his fear that we are losing our awareness of things as concrete values would occur to us only as a vague uneasiness — a feeling that high school should include some requirement that everyone take a course in "art." But with the demands of industry and college entrance boards increasing, it may seem that, except for the talented child, aesthetics is expendable in the interest of greater information and greater facility with the tools of abstract thought. At best, many of us suppose some firsthand contact with painting or music is a nice specialized interest, an enrichment of experience. Yet if Whitehead is right, the ability to elicit sensitive response, "aesthetic vision," is a necessary condition for social progress and for leading a fully human life. The point he is making is, however, that courses in fine arts do not have this effect unless, somehow, the attitude for aesthetic appreciation can transfer, so that we are able to look at the Bayonne refinery, another human being, or a tree as a concrete thing that has intrinsic aesthetic interest and value.

What keeps the rhythmic cycle of education in motion is the lure of value to be obtained. The value cannot all be eventual, however. Life is lived and its various values are concurrently interrelated along lines of a continuous present. The charm of aesthetic value lies in its immediacy, its direct appeal, the significance and flavor that it gives to the present moment. Great art and surpassing natural beauty may have long-term resources that enrich our lives and inspire them as they have the lives of men before us. They may even challenge us to thought and discursive analysis, but the act of aesthetic appreciation is always *now*. Where the element of aesthetic awareness is lost, more complex values have no foundation, and true generality of viewpoint is difficult if not impossible. In short, life is underlived.

How to set about achieving aesthetic awareness is not clear; it probably cannot be programmed in any routine way, since sheer routine is its sworn enemy. Something of the personal quality of the teacher is required; his own habit of sensitivity is contagious. It is a habit learned by individual contact. But the problem illustrates the more general question of sensitivity and authenticity as human qualities that we should teach if we can. It constitutes the final challenge to bring together theoretical philosophy with the practice of education.

II

A Prologue to Future Philosophies of Education

The philosophers we have chosen have the virtue that, among them, they raise a set of questions which must be answered by any adequate philosophy of education. In any inquiry, the first step is exactly this matter of asking the important questions. At the same time, their work shows us that we cannot expect simple, itemized, abstract answers. There are too many interrelated dimensions, too many variations in concrete conditions, for any dogmatic slogan or program to hold the final truth. The history of the idea of education is one of continuing inquiry and discovery. And the philosophy of education requires a constantly creative use of intelligence to create order and value out of the changing human scene.

What are the basic questions we should ask?

1. At the very outset of our discussion, and of the history of the idea of education itself, we face one stubborn and obvious question: Why do we care about education, anyway? What difference does it make to us whether our children are trained by precepts or projects, or whether men a hundred years from now are foolish barbarians? Are we, by some inescapable sensitivity to ideals, attracted by an aim of human progress and betterment? If we are, is there anything in science or psychology that makes this idealism justifiable? And what, more precisely, is the ideal at which we aim? How do we make our children "better" than we are — by removing economic privations and discomforts we have faced, by developing intelligence where we have felt its lack, or in some other way?

2. Whatever may be the "best" analysis of "human nature" (or, if we want to reject this phrase, "the human condition") as we try to clarify the aims of education, it is an unavoidable conclusion that intelligence is an important human power. It is by thinking that we are able to translate ideals into realities, to adapt our environment to what we conceive will be more conducive to survival and progress. Language and mathematics as means of communication and classification, for example, are essential skills if we are ever to recognize order in our experience or connect probable consequences with present decisions. But how does one further the rapid growth of these abilities? Again, in the very beginning of educational theory, we find Plato exploring the value of "mental discipline": of training habits of right, efficient thinking by formal exercises in methods of "thought" or "reasoning" (working out proofs in Euclidean geometry is an example), in the hope that precision and consistency will become general mental habits through such exercise, transferable to any new specific situation. But does this idea work? In his later dialogues Plato seems to have

realized that there is no certainty that intelligence will be developed by purely formal study; apparently he recognized that habits of thought developed in working with one type of problem may have little effect when the problem is of another sort. Great mathematicians are not necessarily or automatically reasonable in their political judgments or theological views. Still, the analogy of "growth" between a physical organism and its "mental powers" is tempting: isn't it true that, by repeated exercise in memorizing, we can strengthen the faculty of memory, much as by squeezing a tennis ball a pitcher can strengthen his grip? And aren't there four or five "faculties" which, working successively, screen out and transmute sense-experiences into "thought?" The idea of growth led Plato's student, Aristotle, to this view of faculties that could be strengthened by selected, specific exercise, and his notions of education included such "mental discipline." This idea has had a long and profound influence on Western educational practice and is still central in Scholastic theories of education. As we read thinkers from ancient times to modern, we repeatedly ask whether there is a real gain in training students to be facile in manipulating symbols to which they can attach little "meaning." And when we look more closely at the classical thinkers who inspired the "discipline" curricula, we may even wonder whether they themselves meant what has been attributed to them. Aristotle puts qualifications into his idea of discipline which are very often close to those that Dewey insists on in the twentieth century.

3. How are growth and maturity both related to education? Shall we think of childhood as a stage of preparation for adult excellence, and therefore give our children the tools and experiences they will find useful later, in adult life? Or should we rather think of childhood as a stage of life that has value in itself for the child, value which must not be sacrificed to uncongenial preparation for some remote future? In either case, we must also ask what the relation is between mental and physical growth, and what role habit and practice, as opposed to insight, have to play in human growing-up. Perhaps the most interesting and significant change in the idea of education between classical and contemporary thought is the change in the con-

cept of "nature" reflected in new thoughts about growth, instinct, science, and maturity.

4. A fourth set of questions, this time about the relation of individuality to social effectiveness, will occur to the contemporary reader who has just finished some such popular book as *The Status Seekers, The Lonely Crowd,* or *The Organization Man*. Does our idea of individualism, coming from British liberal political thought and American frontier life, still apply to society and personality in the twentieth century, or is it out of date? And how do we become socially effective, anyway? Should we learn this in school; if so, can we teach it by courses in history and civics, or must this skill of cooperation in a larger community be learned by actual practice of democratic procedures in the classroom itself? Rousseau, with his story of the education of *Émile*, presents an extreme answer; society is always unnatural, and social adaptation is never a legitimate aim or part of elementary or secondary education, at least for male students. Dewey, working with the immediate background of recent work in evolution and social science, offers an alternative judgment: Without society, there is no individual "self" capable of being authentic. It is, he thinks, as unrealistic to try to think away society in discussing self-realization as it would be to try to analyze respiration apart from any atmosphere.

So far, we have found that before we can understand education we will have to find adequate and realistic (if not precise and forever final) answers to questions about general aims, formal subject matter, maturity and growth, and the relation of the individual to his society. These are not academic questions, made up to puzzle readers. They have immediate practical significance. If one compares Western democracy with its Soviet counterpart, whose civilization challenges our own, it is clear that we must ask the types of questions we have asked. How much should we emphasize social values, how much the individual values? Any local meeting of school board or PTA, any current conversation about education, must be concerned with the same questions.

5. Throughout, we have supposed that our decisions will make some difference, that our students are capable of free

choice and responsible action. Does the notion of human freedom fit in with the findings of science about the order of
nature? The Greek thinkers, who had a feeling for "nature"
as more personal and alive than their Enlightenment successors,
were not deeply concerned with this problem. But when
science seemed, in the seventeenth century, convinced that the
world and everything in it, including ourselves, was part of a
predetermined mechanical order, the question of whether we
are indeed free at all became vital. What sort of explanation
can we give of the apparent fact of total determinism, presented by science, and the inescapable inner awareness of responsibility and freedom of our ethical life? To Kant and
Rousseau it seemed clear that the scientific picture must be
incomplete; but they saw no real alternative to a schizophrenic
separation of man as free and everything else as determined.
Has science since then suggested more plausible answers?
Whether it has or not, do we need two different theories and
sets of goals, depending on whether we are looking at our
students as parts of the world of nature or as strange exceptions
to natural law, possessing an inner dignity that must be elicited
by experience in self-determination? Here we find an apparently irreconcilable gulf between existentialism and logical positivism in the modern scene — and, if we look at it closely and
objectively, an important inconsistency in Marxism. Existentialism implicitly rejects a science of nature as being significant
for human conduct; logical positivism places man squarely *in*
nature and models its methods of analysis of human beings on
those employed by the physical sciences. Marxism regards
man as a complicated end product of the evolutionary development of matter, forgetting that scientific study and theory
comprise but one of many human enterprises which are
experientially on the same footing.

6. A final set of questions occurs, which offers a welcome
change of emphasis. From ancient to contemporary times we
have been concerned with theories and intellectual problems,
or with techniques and the use of intelligence to analyze and
solve practical problems. Is this too intellectualized an approach to the whole question? Can intelligence really operate
effectively apart from aesthetic sensitivity to the world as vivid

and concrete? There is at least a possibility that the ideas of form and control have made us one-sided in our notion of what human existence and experience are. It is one thing to "know" another person by classifying him in some abstract "type": postman, adult male American, the student who sits in the back row — and quite a different thing to "know" someone else as a living, complex human being. If we train our students to unimaginable efficiency in using intelligence to classify and control, to notice the common properties of things that are our clues to the way they will behave, will this really make them "better"? Or would we have left out an equally important part of a good life, an ability to appreciate things as unique individual persons or situations, a direct awareness and sensitivity? If we agree that life has uniqueness, value, vividness, and passion as well as efficiency and objectivity when it is lived well, we still have to ask whether there is any way to teach these other dimensions, in or out of school. Can we do it with courses in art history, with field trips to local industry, with an abstract analysis of "concreteness" in social studies or English courses? Or must we say that human sensitivity, as opposed to skill and intellectual efficiency, cannot be taught? Whitehead and, in a different way, Dewey are typical of our contemporary world in their questioning the classical distinctions of thought and action, intelligence and sensation, freedom and passion, practice and theory.

Plato thought of philosophy as "shared inquiry"; its aim was as much coherence, completeness, and clarity as were possible in the outcome of discussion. In this respect, the situation seems to us unchanged: We would not care to neglect completeness in the interest of a superficial clarity, or to pretend that fixed general answers written in textbooks are really "knowledge"; for knowledge is rather "the living words and ideas in the soul." It is in this spirit that we have tried to study education in the context of philosophy, and that we express our firm belief that no "philosophy of education," ancient or modern, can be adequate unless it asks itself the questions we have been posing, and is sensitive and critical in appraising its answers.

III

CONCLUSION

Our hope is that this book has been a step toward establishing more effective communication and cooperation between experts in education and in philosophy; that it has been interesting in its own right, in showing what a many-faceted and fascinating thing "education" is; and that it will help the reader to meet the difficult demand of thinking about practical educational problems and programs philosophically. It should be clear that our choice is not whether or not to be philosophical, but only whether we are to philosophize well or badly.

Index

Abstraction, 61–62, 181–182
Academy, Plato's, 11, 28, 49, 74
Achilles, Plato's view of, 40
Actual occasion, 174–175, 178
Actuality, as time-structured, 159
Adaptation, as identified with conformity, 189, 195
Adjustment. *See* Adaptation
Administration, problems of, 168
Admiration vs. envy, 86
Adolescence, Émile's, 85–86
Adventures of Ideas, The (Whitehead), 184
Aesthetic form. *See* Esthetic form
Aether, 103
Agathon (good), 21*n*, 25–27, 29
Agathon, the poet, 29
Aims of education. *See* Education, aims of
Aims of Education, The (Whitehead), 163*n*, 164*n*, 165*n*, 167*n*, 168*n*, 169*n*, 170*n*, 171*n*, 176*n*, 177*n*, 178*n*, 179*n*, 180*n*, 183, 184
Ambition, 18
Analogia (analogy), in Plato, 21*n*
Analytics (Aristotle). *See Posterior Analytics*
Antinomies, 107

Anytus, 33
Apology (Plato), 53*n*
Appearance, for Plato, 18
Appearances, as distinct from objects, 106*n*
Appetite, 18
Archē (principle), 56
Ares, 54*n*
Aretē (excellence), 54, 55; and *eudaimonia*, 52–55, 63; intellectual and moral, 54
Aristocratic distinctions, folly of, 85
Aristophanes, 13*n*, 27, 28
Aristotle, 6, 7, 49–75, 76–77, 100, 116, 125, 141, 165, 191, 194; four "causes" of, 56–57 (*See also* Causes); life of, 49; philosophy of education, 50–52; view of art, 69–70; view of childhood, 77; view of curriculum, 67–73; view of growth, 91; view of human nature, 56–58, 59–64; view of nature, 76–77; view of science and education, 57–58; view of theology, 53–54; vs. Plato, 49–50
Art, for Aristotle, 69–70
Association. *See* Habit
Atomic theory, 158
Authenticity, as modern name for nature, 94, 95

199